Respecting Your Limits When Caring for Aging Parents

RESPECTING YOUR LIMITS WHEN CARING FOR AGING PARENTS

VIVIAN E. GREENBERG

Jossey-Bass Publishers • San Francisco

This book is based on my work counseling hundreds of caregivers and their families. To ensure confidentiality, I have changed the names and identifying characteristics of these persons.

Copyright © 1989 by Jossey-Bass Inc., Publishers, 350 Sansome Street, San Francisco, California 94104.

FIRST JOSSEY-BASS PAPERBACK EDITION PUBLISHED IN 1998. THIS BOOK WAS ORIGINALLY PUBLISHED BY LEXINGTON BOOKS.

Substantial discounts on bulk quantities of Jossey-Bass books are available to corporations, professional associations, and other organizations. For details and discount information, contact the special sales department at Jossey-Bass Inc., Publishers (415) 433–1740; Fax (800) 605–2665.

For sales outside the United States, please contact your local Simon & Schuster International Office.

Jossey-Bass Web address: http://www.josseybass.com

Printed in the United States of America

Library of Congress Cataloging-in-Publication Data
Greenberg, Vivian E.
[Your best is good enough]
Respecting your limits when caring for aging parents /
Vivian E. Greenberg. — 1st pbk. ed.
p.   cm.
Originally published: Your best is good enough. Lexington, Mass. :
Lexington Books, ©1989
Includes bibliographical references and index.
ISBN 0-7879-4178-6 (pbk.)
1. Aging parents—Care—United States.   2. Adult children—United
States—Family relationships.   3. Caregivers—United States.
4. Intergenerational relations—United States.   I. Title.
HQ1063.6.G74   1998
306.874—dc21   97-40402
                                                                                    CIP

HB Printing
5 7 9 10 8 6 4
PB Printing
1 3 5 7 9 10 8 6 4 2

This book is dedicated to my father, Arthur Garfing, and especially to the memory of my mother, Minnie Salkin Garfing, for whom my best was good enough.

Contents

Acknowledgements   IX

Introduction   XI

1. The Elder Parent—Adult Child Bond   1

2. What Do Old People Want from Us, Anyway?   9

3. Setting Limits   19

4. Unrealistic Expectations   33

5. Role Reversal   43

6. What about Brothers and Sisters?   51

7. The Manipulative Parent   63

8. Seeing Our Parents as People   71

9. Children without the Gift of Caring   79

10. Who Comes First?   87

11. That Unexplained Anger   99

12. The Hardest Decision of All   105

13. The Second Hardest Decision   119

14. "Difficult" Parents   127

15. Depression and the Elderly   135

16. Honor Thy Father and Mother: Help and Hope   145

    Appendixes   153

    A. Offices on Aging   153

    B. What is a "Professional Geriatric Care Manager"?   155

    C. Levels of Care   157

    D. Family Service America   159

    E. Patient Education Aid   161

    F. Children of Aging Parents (CAPS)   163

    G. Resources for Caregivers   165

    Notes   167

    Index   169

    About the Author   173

Acknowledgments

M Y thanks, first and foremost, to the hundreds of caregivers and their families who, over the years, shared with me their personal struggles and taught me so much about the emotions of caregiving. Without their cooperation and support, this book could not have been written.

To Marianna Fitzpatrick, my longtime friend, who from the outset gave me the confidence to turn a pamphlet into a book, I offer my profound gratitude. Her unflagging encouragement through periods of anxiety and doubt enabled me to finish my manuscript. I am grateful as well to Phyllis O'Connell, whose knowledgeable and insightful suggestions considerably enriched this book.

Others who took time to read my manuscript and make helpful comments were: Dixie Anderson, Ann T. Crystal, Michelle Galie, and Stanley Glick. To all, my sincere thanks.

To Scott Paist III, M.D., director of the Family Medicine Residency Program of Memorial Hospital of Burlington County, Mount Holly, New Jersey, and Christine Wanich, R.M., M.S.N., of the University of Pennsylvania, my colleagues on the geriatric assessment team of Memorial Hospital, I express my appreciation for the opportunity to share knowledge from our diverse fields. Our work together from 1983 to 1986 added a holistic dimension to my understanding of the elderly.

To my sons, Bruce and Bob Rosenthal, my gratitude and thanks— to one for his editing assistance and to the other for his help in translating pertinent psychiatric concepts into readable language.

To Joyce Miller of the Burlington County Office on Aging, my thanks for necessary information.

To my typists, Betty Serfass and Arlene Poreda, I am deeply grateful not only for a job well done but also for their patience and graciousness during stressful moments.

To my colleagues and friends Barbara Bristow, LCSW, member of the board of directors of the National Association of Professional Geriatric Care Managers, and Janice McCurdy, LCSW, my thanks for their valuable contributions to the paperback edition and for their overall support.

And to Louise Fradkin and Mirca Liberti, founders of CAPS (Children of Aging Parents), my deepest gratitude for their ongoing interest in and support of my work.

Finally to Stan, my staunchest support, who from his big, red chair was always ready to listen to an idea, read a paragraph, or reassure me with a gentle word, my thanks and my love.

Introduction

MORE than ten years have passed since I wrote the first edition of this book. While this decade has spawned a greater consciousness of aging and caregiving, resulting in more public and private resources for adults who are caring for their elderly parents, the stresses for those in the throes of caregiving have not lessened. Caregivers, still mostly daughters and daughters-in-law, feel overwhelmed and torn by conflicting emotions. They try to do more than they realistically can for their elderly parents but fear they are not doing enough. They feel angry and resentful toward their parents for the demands they make upon them yet feel guilty and ashamed over what they perceive as selfishness when their parents cannot be first on their agenda of responsibilities. And they find it difficult to balance the needs of their parents with the needs of their families and their own needs for rest and recreation. By the time these beleaguered people come to see me for guidance, they are stressed beyond their limits—burned out—and their caregiving relationships with their parents have escalated to crisis proportions.

As a clinical social worker with twenty-three years of experience in geriatrics and caregiving, I do not see the pressures on families to give long-term care to their parents decreasing as we enter the twenty-first century. In 1987, when I first began to write this book, Children of Aging Parents (CAPS) was the only information, support, and referral group for caregivers. Today National Family Caregivers Association in Kensington, Maryland, serves a similar purpose. Whereas in 1987, CAPS sponsored five local caregivers support groups, today there are twenty-five CAPS groups throughout the United States. Magazines, like *Answers* and *The Sandwich Generation*, written expressly to help adult children cope during the parent-care years, are currently part of the resource pool to assist caregivers. Indeed, from the *Wall Street Journal* to the *New Age Journal* to *Town and*

Country, articles abound about the stresses of caring for elderly parents. Even corporate America has responded to the pleas of caregivers for assistance. Beginning in 1988, companies like Stride Rite, IBM, Merck, AT&T, 3M and Unisys developed and implemented a variety of on-site services for employees caring for elderly parents.

I am certain that in the decades to come, as government spends less on the care of the elderly and with care provided through a capitation (fixed fee per individual per month) system, there will be even more support groups, magazines, and information/referral services to help families. I watch with avid interest those extraordinary agents of change, the baby boomers; I wonder what innovative programs they will come up with as they become elders and look to *their* children for support.

Make no mistake, as long as there are families children will want to honor their elderly parents with care. It is quite simply the nature of the bond. In the 1980s, the late sociologist, Christopher Lasch (see page 6), rebuked us for being a culture of narcissism. In the 1990s, we have William Bennett of the American Enterprise Institute to remind us of the demise of family values. But in the arena of giving care to our elderly parents, neither narcissism nor family irresponsibility has even a toehold.

As a result of the pleas I have heard from hundreds of families, I wrote this practical and direct book about what I have learned to recognize as the common problems adults face while caring for their parents. With each chapter focusing on a specific area, it is a fairly short guide which the caregiver can reach for when she or he feels helpless and hopeless. It addresses the anger, guilt, frustration, and sadness caregivers experience as they give the best care they can to their elderly parents. If heeded, this book can bring joy to children, and in turn to their parents, as they give care.

What kinds of families do I write about? I don't write about so-called sick families, eroded by years of hatred and emotional distance, where children are determined to avenge past hurts and grievances by behaving in cruel and sometimes violent ways toward their parents. Elder abuse—"granny bashing"—is a horrible reality. Some states, like Virginia, have taken brisk action to combat the problem by establishing elder abuse prevention coalitions. Nor do I address the pain and hurt experienced by families where a parent or spouse has Alzheimer's disease. Many outstanding books and articles on this subject are available to those who need them. State Alzheimer's Associations, not on the scene in 1987, are today the premier resource for information about any facet of the illness and its management.

My focus will be the overwhelmed middle-aged adults whom I refer to in another book as "children of a certain age." Caught between the demands of their aging parents and their own families, they constitute an ever-growing and ever-graying army of caregivers. Leading the front line is a phalanx of older daughters, described by Elaine Brody of the Philadelphia Geriatric Center as the "women in the middle."

Whether in conversations with friends or sessions with clients, the questions and pleas from these caring children in 1997 are identical to those a decade earlier. "What can I do about my eighty-five-year-old mother who refuses to get household help?" "How can I make my parents understand that I can't be with them all the time?" "How can I make myself understand that I cannot be with them all the time without feeling that I should be?" "It's not fair that my sister doesn't lift a finger to help; I work more hours than she does." "My brother could at least call our parents once a week instead of once a year." "I feel so guilty about leaving Dad for a week, but if I don't get away I'll go crazy." "My parents complain bitterly about their Meals-On-Wheels dinner, but I can't cook for them every day; I work and have my own family to cook for." "Between running to my Dad's before work and returning after work and then taking care of my own family, I feel my life is haywire. But I can't stop. I don't know how!" "It's obvious my parents can no longer remain in their apartment, but they refuse to leave. How do I handle this?"

"I'm beginning to get angry about sacrificing so much of my scarce leisure time to my mother's incessant demands. I know it's wrong to be angry at her, but I can't help it." "My mother is always depressed since my father died. I try to entertain her and bring interest to her life, but nothing helps. Can anything be done for her?" "It's so scary and depressing to watch my father become an angry old man. If I'm that way at eighty, I'll take a pill." "My mother puts such a guilt trip on me by telling me I owe her all the care she gave me as a child. That's not so, is it?" The issues and questions are raised with intense urgency. There isn't a day that passes without someone with one of these problems calling or coming in for help.

* * *

With knowledge and understanding about what is taking place within us and within our parents as we interact in the caregiving experience, we will acquire the know-how to be less stressed, happier caregivers. This knowledge, uncomplicated and common sense in its approach, can be applied to those areas where we feel stuck. Just as there are guidelines to help people through widowhood, divorce and bereavement, there are strategies and techniques to enable adults to navigate the troubled waters of generational conflict with their elderly parents. Certain patterns between parent and adult child are difficult to change; some patterns may never change. Even what is resistant to change, however, can be transformed into a more manageable solution. Some seemingly hard-core situations often improve with merely a better understanding of our expectations and those of our parents. Because we are determined to make our final years with our parents positive, we can easily learn what has to be learned.

As you read this book, you will find that in many instances what you expect of yourself is more than you can realistically give. If you turn down the dial a notch or two on your self-imposed "expectationstat," you will be able to reduce the tension and anguish in your life. Although we all know the value of straight, honest talk in improving intimate relationships, emotional barriers exist that prevent us from applying those communication principles to our interactions with our elderly parents. Understanding those barriers is also what this book is about.

Today there is more help than ever for adults who are trying to be dependable caregivers to their elderly parents. And there's more to come as we and our parents live longer and healthier (also sicker) lives. Although we have come a long way since 1965, when the Older Americans Act became law, establishing offices on aging in every county in the United State (see Appendix A), we are still behind other western countries in providing respite services to caregivers.

Most adults take on the responsibilities of caregiving without fuss or protest: they genuinely want to honor their parents in their last years. They also have a right to personal happiness and well being, which does not have to be at the expense of their parents' welfare. There is a way to balance the needs of both generations, so that we can *take* care while *giving* care.

What has not changed since 1987 is that I am still taking care of my father. At ninety-four, he has resided in a nursing home for almost three years. He resides in a "good" home close to where I live and I see him often. What I feel about nursing homes and the need for "good" ones I say in chapter 12. The only difference is that since I have been through the experience of *placing* a parent, I now believe what I wrote even more.

* * *

For "children of a certain age," their parents' old age brings home for the first time the somber realization that they too will grow old and die. Until that time when we notice the signs of old age in our parents, we live in a never-never land where we believe that we and our parents will remain as we are. With our parents' decline and need for care, our fantasy of immortality is blown: one day our parents will die, and we will grow old and die too. It's a strange thing, this irrational feeling we have that as long as our parents are alive we are protected from death.

The notion that our lives are finite is made more poignant by the physical changes that unrelentingly intrude upon the awaited joys of mid-life. Middle age, the precursor of old age, tests us with lessened physical capacity as well as an increased risk for illness. A friend has open heart surgery; another is diagnosed with Parkinson's disease; another shows signs of osteoporosis; and yet another loses a wife to cancer. At times, sadly, we feel as old as our parents! Some of us in our sixties and seventies may, indeed, be sicker or more infirm than our parents, and some of us may not outlast them.

Let's face it, we are called upon to give care to our parents when we ourselves are running out of steam; we cannot do all that we thought we could. In such instances, expectations must be altered and painful decisions must be made as we balance and sort out the critical variables that affect our individual caregiving situation. It is the defining and redefining of those expectations that makes the difference between caregiving as joy and caregiving as stress. We do have a choice.

1

The Elder Parent–Adult Child Bond

THE call usually begins with, "I'm really worried about my mother. She's eighty, was just discharged from the hospital after her second fall, and won't allow me to get help for her. What shall I do? I'm being torn to pieces." Or, "My seventy-seven-year-old mother is really impossible. She's been living with me for four years. I have a part-time job three days per week which I must keep, and now she blocks the door every morning, shouting that if I loved her I would stay home. I have two sisters nearby who want to help out but she won't let them. She only wants me. For God's sake, what shall I do?" The caller is usually an adult daughter; the presenting problem is usually an elderly mother. A son may also call and a father too may be the subject, but four out of five times, as I've counted, it has been the former situation.

Sometimes the tone in the caller's voice will be sad rather than exasperated. For example, a sixty-five-year-old daughter phoned to ask if I knew of someone who could stay with her mother for a few days so she and her husband could get away for a short vacation. The last six years of their twenty-eight-year marriage were marked with her widowed mother's presence in their home. Her mother suffered a stroke one year after moving in with her, then her husband had heart bypass surgery. The daughter's retirement as a school teacher coincided with her father dying and her mother moving in with them. She is an only child, her husband also has no siblings, and because they married late in life they decided not to have children. She described her mother as "always needing a lot of attention, which my long-suffering father gave her, but my time is running out and my husband and I need to get away. My mother will be in a rage, but I'm in a rage too. My mother tells me that if we leave her for a few days she'll die. What can I do? I don't have the strength I once had."

And so it goes. Calls from loving, well-intentioned middle-aged children, all bursting with feelings of helplessness, anger, and frustration that seem to be part of the process of caring for an aging parent, continue to pour in.

Adult children are involved in taking care of their parents to an extent unprecedented in our history. As Elaine Brody[2] has so clearly pointed out, adult children today administer the most difficult personal care to their aging parents and do so at considerable cost to their own health and welfare. Moreover, they do everything within their power to keep parents in their homes as long as possible. Adult children consider the option of nursing home placement only as a final alternative and then experience deep pain and grief when their parent makes the final move. Psychologists have postulated, and I agree, that the grief reaction of an adult child after placing a parent in a nursing home is more intense than what is felt after that parent dies. "Those good old days," as Brody refers to them, when those who would like to distort reality say children *really* took care of their parents, never existed. Logic dictates that those good old days never existed, simply because people didn't live that long. With only 6 percent of those over sixty-five in nursing homes and 84 percent of elder care in this country administered by family members, the multi-generational home is a thing of the present. Three generations who share the same household or who live within an hour of one another are more likely to live in split-level homes in suburban Philadelphia or Cleveland than in little houses on the prairie.

Although adult children have always cared for their elderly parents, the term *sandwich generation* is a "now" phenomenon in every sense. At the turn of the century, before women had careers, worked because their paychecks were required for more than luxuries, or were single heads of households, they were not squeezed between generational layers as they are today. The pull on caregivers, whether married or single, is unprecedented in our social history. The conflicts and stresses associated with caring for our elderly parents are new problems requiring new solutions and strategies. If, as predicted, by the year 2030, one out of five people in our country will be over sixty-five, the difficulties we currently experience may be minuscule compared to what they will be then. These staggering demographic statistics, combined with such major sociologic changes as the increasing divorce rate, smaller families, remarried families, and families without children, augur for complexities and stumbling blocks, the magnitude of which we can only imagine. Indeed, the graying of America in the twenty-first century may be one of government's greatest challenges, in terms of creating human resources to care compassionately for elderly people without families.

The increased longevity resulting from medical advances and heightened know-how regarding how to take care of ourselves has been a double-edged sword. Though the young-old (sixty-five to seventy-five years of age) are healthier than ever, the old-old (eighty-five to ninety-five) are able to live longer with their chronic illnesses. It is no longer a rarity to see a seventy-year-old daughter visiting her ninety-two-year-old mother in a nursing home. Nor is it unusual to see a sixty-year-old daughter using a cane while her seventy-nine-year-old mother is able to walk without one. One member of my support group has had two hip replacements while her eighty-nine-year-old mother's hips are in perfect condition. If one out of ten caregivers to an aging parent in this country is over sixty-five, the health and stamina of the caregiver must become a factor in determining how much care he or she can render.

As a student social worker, I once gasped in disbelief when a colleague told me about an eighty-five-year-old mother who was caring for her sixty-five-year-old widowed, stroke-damaged daughter. I remember being told about a ninety-one-year-old mother who, when she heard her seventy-two-year-old daughter screaming on the front porch, came out armed with a broom and shooed away a would-be burglar. I am no longer shocked by such stories. Both combinations of caregiving are possible as we reach the year 2000, when one out of ten persons in the United States will be over sixty-five. In fact, currently the health fields are giving much necessary attention to aging parents who are caring for their disabled, infirm children. The focus of this book, however, will be on the more usual caregiving situation of adult child caring for aging parents.

Although the myth that adult children neglect their elderly parents has been thoroughly discredited by solid scientific evidence, I am amazed by the large number of people who still persist in believing that adult children really do not care and dump their elderly parents in boarding or nursing homes. How many times has someone said to me, "I think it's a disgrace the way children treat their parents today."? Having worked with old people and their families in nursing homes, boarding homes, life-care communities, hospitals, outpatient mental health and medical clinics, medical day-care centers, and in their homes, I can unequivocally say that if the myth is not dead, it deserves to be.

Every old person I have seen in these settings has had at least one adult child concerned with his welfare. The range of concern varies from very active, with children who engage in a variety of supportive and instrumental services on a daily basis, to minimally active, with children who limit their support to phone calls. In between are those adult children who see their parents most weekends and phone every day; those who are available only for emergencies and call rarely; those who do the weekly marketing and engage in little parental socialization; those who see their parents once per year during vacation from work but call frequently; and those who serve only as central control boards to arrange and monitor community services, preferring to avoid intense emotional involvement. The combinations of caregiving are obviously endless, depending upon the emotional closeness of the family and the health, age, job, and other responsibilities of the primary caregiver.

Each family is unique in terms of its composition, nature of family relationships, attitudes, and values. Because the nuclear family is no longer the predominate family form in America, the term *family* itself must be clearly defined. Within the context of giving care to elderly parents, family form is a crucial factor. Contrast the commitment of a spouse to an elderly parent-in-law in a newly created (five years) remarried family with that of a spouse in a thirty-five-year marriage, where in-laws have a long history of involvement with grandchildren and general sharing in family celebrations, milestones, and crises. Is it fair or realistic to expect spouses in remarried families to demonstrate the same level of care and emotional investment as spouses in long-term, one-time marriages? Spouses in remarried families are faced with the additional monumental job of building a new family.³ The impact of this major task on the caregiving experience was poignantly explained in one of our support group meetings by a thirty-seven-year-old caregiver married to a forty-eight-year-old man with two children.

> We've been married for four years. We share custody of my husband's two teenage daughters and we have a year-and-a-half-old son of our own. Every ounce of energy I have is needed to forge us into a new, cohesive family. All went well until my mother died and my father suffered a stroke. I am an only child. Though I love my father, his needs are secondary to those of my family. If you wish to judge me selfish for making this decision, I will try to understand. I do not, however, think it fair that I should be expected to give as much to my dad as some of you who are a part of a long marriage, where your children have already left the nest.

Or what about Emily's situation? She is a forty-seven-year-old widow who suffers from a serious chronic gastrointestinal disease (one that cannot be cured and depletes her supply of physical and psychic energy). How much should she be expected to give, both emotionally and in terms of concrete services, like grocery shopping and transportation, to her eighty-one-year-old mother? Imagine her sadness and guilt because she cannot care for her as she would like.

Consider, too, families in which relationships between parents and children are characterized by coolness and distance. Not all parents and children are fortunate enough to love or even like one another (see chapter 9). Should children from these families be expected to care for their elderly parents to the same degree and in the same manner as children from loving, close families?

In the case of children and parents separated by a continent or even an ocean, adult children call often, fly out several times during the year if they are able, and know that in a pinch they can be with a parent in a matter of a few hours. I have counseled adult children with elderly parents in South Africa, Germany, Finland, Israel, and England. These adult children experience the same emotions as children whose parents live nearby. If anything, their pain and guilt are intensified by feelings of helplessness resulting from the vast geographic space that separates them from their mothers and fathers.

Of note, too, is the emergence of a new kind of long-distance caregiving, in which a social worker or professional with a graduate degree in human services serves as care manager and liaison for the concerned adult child who lives too far away to be active in the care of his parent. Nonprofit and for-profit care management services have sprung up throughout the country, particularly in the Northeast and in Florida. Information on geriatric care managers can be obtained by writing to: the National Association of Professional Geriatric Care Managers, 1604 North Country Club Road, Tucson, Arizona 85716, (520) 881-8008.*

A care manager arranges for necessary supports such as home-health aides, transportation services, and shopping. Additionally, she has at her fingertips an up-to-date assessment of how father or mother is managing in his or her home. The adult child and the care manager keep in constant touch, so that the adult child can have almost total information concerning the medical, social, and emotional condition of his parent. Although such services can be costly, they lessen the feelings of helplessness and guilt generated by insurmountable physical distance. Said an adult son, for whom I serve as care manager to his parents, "What a relief, Vivian, to know that you are there; that I can call you whenever I wish to find out how Mom and Dad are doing. Through you, I know I am taking care of my parents." My services as care manager are given under the auspices of Jewish Family Service of the Delaware Valley, an accredited, non-profit family service agency. More will be said about the nature of these services in chapter 13.

The very existence of care management services attests to the willingness and capacity of adult children to provide the best possible care for their elderly parents. Likewise, the reverse migration of elderly parents away from their Florida homes back to where their children live validates the strength of the elder parent-adult child bond. Though times and families have dramatically changed, the conduct of most caregivers is still governed by old rules of what children owe their parents in terms of care. "Me second, Mom first" remains the credo for the majority of caregivers. However popular the social and economic philosophies advanced by social scientists Christopher Lasch[4] and Daniel Yankelovich,[5] that Americans are en-

---

*For a fuller description of the services of the National Association of Professional Geriatric Care Managers, see appendix B.

gaged in the pursuit of their own self-fulfillment, the commitment of adult children to their elderly parents offers viable evidence that at least in one sector of our society individuals are pursuing altruistic goals: honoring their mothers and fathers.

2

What Do Old People Want from Us, Anyway?

M ANY a client has said to me, "My mother won't let me do a thing for her. It's just maddening, because I could make life so much more comfortable for her." The truth is that old people generally want to do as much as they can for as long as they can by themselves and for themselves. An adult daughter I know has finally accepted her father's wish to do the dishes by himself. Whenever she arrives at his apartment, she immediately wants to plunge into the stack of dirty dishes sitting in the sink. This eighty-five-year-old father is in pretty good health, although understandably slower than he once was, and enjoys doing the dishes alone after she leaves. He tells her, "Sit and talk to me; you didn't come here to be my maid." This last statement is a clear metaphor for what elderly parents truly want from their adult children.

Certainly it would be easier for an adult son to come to his parents' home to do some dusting and cleaning. Easier for whom, however? In many instances, easier for him, not for his mother. As old people are able to manage fewer of the tasks of daily living and must depend on others to perform them, whatever they can still do by themselves assumes enormous significance. Polishing the brass candlesticks and peeling and coring apples to make a big pot of applesauce are precious symbols of control and independence. So what if these activities take an hour longer! One elderly gentleman I know preferred using a weekly senior transportation service to the doctor to accepting his son's most willing offer to perform the same service. This father would say to me, "Taking care of myself in this way makes me feel as if I'm still a real person—someone who counts, not just a zero."

The metaphoric statement, "sit and talk to me; you didn't come here to be my maid," sums up precisely what old people want from their children. They want to feel secure in the knowledge that their children will be there for them emotionally. What does it mean to be there emotionally for someone? It simply means that you will be there to listen to that person when she feels like talking. That you will say, "I understand," when that person says she's feeling depressed and down—not "I'm sure you'll feel better tomorrow; it's probably something you ate." The therapeutic effect of listening— real, "active" listening, when you are completely focused upon the talker—can never be understated. To intensely listen to what someone says conveys in the most powerful way possible that you care deeply for that person and accept that person for what she is without qualification. As old people lose more and more of their friends and acquaintances, who is left to whom they can talk and who will listen to them? Adult children with whom they have shared so many years and common experiences are the ones to fill that deep void.

It is not necessary to visit or call a parent every day to demonstrate that you care about and love her. We're talking about quality and not quantity of time spent. The affect—the feeling—that permeates the encounter between parent and adult child is what really matters. Daily telephone conversations made routinely and out of a sense of obligation are worth less than a one-half-hour exchange in which your parent and you warmly share a funny time that took place twenty years ago when you all went to the beach together. That your widowed father can feel secure knowing you won't react with annoyance and impatience to his call that he's feeling a little lonely is "being with him emotionally."

Of course, daily phone calls serve a significant purpose and I do not mean to trivialize them. I call my father just about every morning before I go to work. He loves to hear from me and I love to hear his voice. But seeing a ball game with your father on television on a Sunday afternoon or reminiscing with your mother about the weekend you visited your son in college indicates to your parents that you still enjoy them and find them good company. Such "close encounters" validate to your parents that they still count in your eyes—the most important eyes of all. And when that time comes when your mother and father are no longer with you, these moments will furnish the memories to sustain you and to bring you the unique comfort that you were a good son or daughter. Perhaps the most practical fringe benefit resulting from quality meetings, however, is the lessening of those odd-hour phone calls that drive you crazy. When parents feel that their children are emotionally with them their anxiety about being abandoned and not cared for will diminish.

Let me say outright, however, that quality time spent with parents does not guarantee that your parents will *always* feel secure and cared for. Your parents and most old people will feel anxious and lonely from time to time. They will think that nobody really cares whether they survive or not. *Such feelings and thoughts seem to come with the territory of old age, so don't take them personally.* How easy it is to respond to such feelings of despondency as though we were their cause. Taught from childhood to be sensitive to the emotional temperature of others, women especially are ready to jump into the ring not only to assume responsibility for others' painful feelings but to rescue those others from whatever ill fate awaits. Remember, these are natural feelings that old people experience and you are not responsible for them. Most elderly people are capable of working them out for themselves; they have lived as long as they have because they are survivors and "copers." If you have the kind of parent who is comfortable talking about feelings, then you are in a position to help by listening and interjecting supportive, caring comments. If not, do not rush in to rescue. Be patient and, of course, show concern by letting your parent know that you sense this is a painful period and that you are available for whatever help she needs.

The accumulation of so many losses—health, vigor, friends, income—in so short a period of time, which renders the old person dependent on others, may account for the abandonment anxiety that she experiences. These feelings are further intensified by the attitudes of our society, which in its values and actions writes off old people as worthless and useless. When age spots are called ugly and most media presentations are geared to the tastes of the young, how can the old feel valued and cared for? How can they not feel abandoned and insecure no matter how attentive and caring their adult children are?

Although it is difficult to predict when parents may experience these intense feelings of abandonment, there are periods when they seem to be most vulnerable. Let me list several.

1. Upon discharge from the hospital, a parent may feel anxious and alone.

2. Before an adult child leaves on vacation, a parent may feel anxious, worrying that he may not be able to manage without that child's help. That parent may, additionally, fear that his child might be in an accident and won't come back at all.

3. After a lovely warm evening spent with family and friends, a widowed parent may feel abandoned and alone upon returning to her empty apartment. She may reach for the phone to call you.

4. If for some reason, an adult child is not able to make that routine weekly visit or daily phone call, a parent may feel the adult child does not care, resulting in feelings of abandonment.

5. If an adult child becomes ill, requires surgery, or is hurt in an accident, the parent will feel abandonment anxiety. In such situations these feelings may be the most intense.

6. During holiday seasons, especially Thanksgiving and Christmas, the parent may feel abandoned and isolated even though he or she is included in every family celebration.

Knowing when our parents may become anxious is the first step. Knowing what to say during these instances is the second.

Many times when our parents are frightened, thinking no one cares or will be there to help them when needed, they will disguise their grievance in the form of a physical complaint. An adult daughter, whose mother was recently discharged from the hospital after cardiac catheterization, called me one morning to tell me her mother was driving her up a wall. She would call at the oddest hours (8:30 A.M. before the daughter was to leave for work, or 12:00 A.M. while the daughter was in bed) with vague complaints about feeling dizzy or "my stomach doesn't exactly hurt, but it feels strange lower down." The calls were persistent and the daughter truly felt that her mother had "flipped" and was ready for long-term placement in a skilled care facility.

We explored the problem together and the daughter was able to understand that her mother was feeling frightened. Her mother was neither a manipulative woman nor a hypochondriac; she did not deliberately couch her complaints in physical terms to get attention. This was the only way she could communicate her helplessness to her daughter. The communication took place on a level the mother did not understand. With the daughter's understanding of her mother's inner turmoil, she eventually responded with, "Mom, I know how scared you are being home from the hospital after such a serious procedure. I'm sure you must hurt all over. I would love to really talk to you, but you just woke my husband and me; I am tired and this is not the time to talk. I'll call you tomorrow morning when I have a few minutes and we'll arrange to go out to lunch or something, just the two of us. Okay?"

The daughter was able to say this without anger and resentment. She voiced her needs without devaluing Mother's. Old people are very sensitive to the verbal and nonverbal cues of rejection. Any hint of exasperation or annoyance, even over the telephone, will be registered by the parent. In face-to-face confrontations, however, it is easier to communicate acceptance and support of your parent's feelings. A caress of the shoulder or a squeeze of the hand will transmit that you care and understand. Of course, the genuine understanding of your parent's needs is the basis for the caring tone you convey. You cannot convey a caring tone if you do not feel it or if you are angry. Sometimes it may become necessary to consult with a counselor to help you sort out your emotions when your parent's abandonment anxiety interferes with your daily life. Persistent intrusions by parents at inappropriate times will cause resentment and subsequent guilt over that resentment. Said one daughter, "My mother keeps calling with her demands. I get angry and hang up in a huff, then feel guilty and call her back to apologize for my insensitivity. Then she begins again with her complaints and I'm angry all over again." The cycle of anger, guilt, anger is hard to break. If you are feeling confused and stuck, call a counselor or join a support group. To do nothing will only aggravate an already stressful experience.

Most aging parents I have spoken to truly want their grown children to prosper and enjoy their lives. My eighty-four-year-old father encourages my husband and me to live fully, saying "What do you think that you are going to go and do when you are my age? Now's the time to do things, when you have the energy and health." In fact, the healthier and happier you are, the more secure your parents will feel. The feelings of abandonment and helplessness mentioned earlier may reach their peak when a parent observes poor health or illness in an adult child. The fear that something could happen to an adult child is totally overwhelming. Not only is anxiety generated by worry that there will be no one to care for them, but the notion that "something bad can happen to my child and not to me" devastates their sense of how things should be in this world. As the natural order of life's events, parents expect incapacity, decline, and death for themselves but not for their children until long after they have gone. The utter helplessness and despair experienced by aging parents when their children face tragedy have no limits. With increased longevity for our parents and ourselves at an all-time high, the possibility that parents may witness illness and even death in their children becomes a sad reality.

What do old people want from us, anyway? When they are not mentally impaired, they want to be part of any decision made about their lives. I am reminded of the time an adult son came to see me because his sister had taken away the keys to his mother's car without consulting her. Mother was getting forgetful and had had an accident about two weeks before the son called. The son told me on the telephone that "the keys to the car are the keys to my mother's independence." Apparently one of the few pleasures left to this elderly lady was a daily drive of two miles to a shopping mall where she would eat lunch, browse through the stores, sit on a bench for a while to watch passers-by, and then return to her apartment in a senior residence development. By the time the son came to see me, he had found out that "the accident" consisted of Mother's lightly bumping a parked car in the driveway of the building where she lived. He went on to say that his mother was so depressed and distraught because she didn't have her car that he wondered if it was worth taking away her keys. He wanted to return the keys to her, telling me he felt it was worth the risk. What did I think? I agreed and we decided upon two things. First, he would tell Mother she would regain the use of her car and apologize for taking the keys away without discussing the matter with her. Second, because he and his sister were worried about her increasing forgetfulness, he hoped she would agree to a complete geriatric evaluation to determine if her memory impairment could become a serious problem. She consented to the latter and is still driving to her beloved mall to this day, as far as I know. The lessons to be learned from this story are that adult children must respect their parents' need for independence, even if it involves allowing a parent to take a risk, and that any decision about a parent's life should be made with that parent's full participation.

What is a symbol of independence for one elderly person may not be for another. For the woman of seventy-five whose identity is inextricably linked to her ability to prepare marvelous meals for her family, her life will continue to have meaning as long as she can still put something tasty on the table. For the eighty-year-old man, who was a certified accountant and took pride in his talent with numbers, the fact that he can still balance his checkbook means he is not over-the-hill.

What I have found to be an almost universal symbol of independence among the elderly is, believe it or not, the automobile. Elderly persons I have worked with will hang on to their cars even though they are fully aware that their driving days are over. The car may sit in the parking lot or garage of their apartment building, only to be warmed up for several minutes each month, but this doesn't matter as long as the car is there. An adult son whose father lives on the tenth floor of a retirement high-rise told me his father will not allow him to sell his car. Even though he knows he can never drive again, he likes to see it from his window first thing each morning and the feel of the keys in his pocket makes him feel terrific.

The rise of life care communities in this country additionally attests to the strong desire of elderly persons to do it on their own. These facilities are staffed and equipped to meet the medical, personal, social, and cultural needs of their residents until death. They provide intermediate, personal, and skilled nursing care,* when these become necessary. As long as a resident is in good health, he can engage in a variety of activities and interests ranging from movies, concerts, and lectures to religious services, arts and crafts, and gardening. Life care communities have libraries, auditoriums, gyms, health clinics, and even greenhouses. An elegantly appointed dining room serves three gourmet meals daily and a van provides transportation to shopping malls, restaurants, theaters, and so on. As resi-

---

*See appendix C for a fuller description of care levels.

dents become frail, they progress to the above-mentioned care levels. If a spouse becomes ill, for example, the well spouse does not have to travel far to visit. An elevator ride to another floor or a short walk to another building enables the healthy spouse to make daily, stress-free visits. Additionally, and of more importance, the well spouse will not experience the terrible loneliness that comes with the absence of a mate. He is able to dine and mingle with others and not give up fulfilling activities and interests.

Parents who are fortunate enough to live in these communities do not have to call upon their children to transport them here and there, to market for them, to take them to doctors' appointments, or to find companions and home-health aides for them. Parents who live in life care communities are able to be independent, obtaining for themselves necessary services. They do not make demands on their children! Consequently, as one adult daughter put it, "Visits with my mom and dad are a pleasure. My husband and I visit every week for dinner. We have marvelous conversations and we all enjoy one another very much." Unfortunately, life care communities are expensive and limited to those who have means. For a couple, they can cost a minimum of $65,000 (called a founder's fee) for entry and $700 per month for maintenance. Entry fees can run as high as $250,000 and maintenance as high as $3,000. (A valuable guide to life-care communities is *If I Live to be 100*, by Vivian F. Carlin, Ph.D., and Ruth Mansberg [Princeton, N.J.: Princeton Book Co., 1989].) Rental retirement communities, although not offering the luxuries of "buy-ins," are more reasonable in cost and do provide interesting and diverse activities. What they lack, however, are the levels of nursing care. Many of my contemporaries are considering these total care communities in planning for their own old age. Not surprisingly, the primary reason for this choice is the imperative: "I shall not, in my old age, be a burden to my children."

In addition to total life care communities, an array of other living options abound which allow parents independence and flexibility. Retirement hotels and residential health care and adult congregate living facilities offer residents private or semi-private rooms with bath, housekeeping services, three nutritious meals daily, and activities programs. Those worth considering are licensed by the state to meet rigid standards for the safety and health of their residents. Generally the larger the facility, the more amenities and activities are provided. Capacity may range from eight persons in small group homes to over two hundred in larger, high-rise buildings. Some of these facilities supply twenty-four-hour nursing care; most are within easy access to health services. A number of larger facilities provide pull cords and in-house telephones in each room in case of emergency. Transportation for shopping, entertainment, and doctors' appointments is always offered. Lounges, libraries, playrooms for visiting grandchildren, solariums, billiard rooms, beauty parlors, and barber shops are standard fixtures in the more affluent facilities.

To qualify for admission, the applicant must be in reasonably good health. Some facilities require a physician's certificate stating that the person is not in need of hospital care. These facilities do not provide intermediate care for infirm adults who require extra supervision of medical needs, but have on hand appropriate staff to assist with personal care—that is, bathing, dressing, personal hygiene, and medication. Monthly rates range from $500 to $1,500, depending upon the size and nature of the facility. Listings of these facilities can be obtained from your state Office on Aging and state Department of Human Services.

Because a parent is old does not mean he can no longer think. Frequently, adult children feel that old age marks either the beginning of a process or the end of one, I'm not sure which, where their parents can no longer act rationally. Some years ago, I was asked by a member of my support group to speak with his adult daughter who felt that he should not be taking care of his wife, her mother, who had Alzheimer's. Although my client was seventy-eight years old he had the vigor and health to perform the difficult care required and the good judgment to know his limitations. The daughter, refusing to acknowledge her father's unusual capacity to give, constantly badgered him to put Mother in a nursing home. She would tell him over and over again, "Dad, you really don't know what you're doing!" It was decided that the father should bring his daughter to one of our support group meetings. There, the other members, over a period of time, helped her to perceive her father as quite capable and to understand that it is her father's right to care for his wife if this is what he chooses to do. When she accepted these facts, she was able to have a much closer relationship with her father and to be more supportive of his efforts to care for her mother at home.

Elderly parents generally want to feel that they are valued and loved by their grown children. What they want from their children more than the ride to the doctor's or supermarket is to know that their children still want to be with them and hear what they have to say. Aging parents want to feel they are part of and have an important place in the family; that they are appreciated and respected by their children and grandchildren for what they can still contribute to their lives in the way of wisdom and experience. Aging parents want to be asked what *they* think about this or that event or topic. They want to be included in family discussions and family business. They want to know what's going on, whether it be good or bad. To hide a grandchild's divorce, for example, for fear that your parent won't be able to cope with the shock, is to invalidate your parent as a thinking, feeling human being. To exclude a parent from such a major happening is to render that parent a nonperson. Healthy elderly parents, like all healthy people, want to be part of—not outside of—a network of caring, loving persons. What aging parents fear most is isolation from the bustle of family life and activity. Grown children can give their parents this valuable connection.

3

Setting Limits

L ET'S get back to that first phone call mentioned in chapter 1: the distressed, frustrated daughter who cannot convince her mother that get necessary household help. It seems her mother has Parkinson's disease and her most recent fall, one of many, resulted in hospitalization. This mother is what we term "high risk" (for further injuries or hospitalization). She needs help but will not allow her daughter to make the necessary support arrangements upon her discharge home. She refuses homemakers and rejects the idea of adding a bathroom downstairs and turning the dining room into a bedroom. "Money is not an impediment," cries the daughter, "only her stubbornness." She goes on:

My mother has always been domineering and now my brother and I know what my father went through. She has had home-health aides, but none was good enough for her. She complained about each one. This one left a dish in the sink; that one didn't like her, etc. And besides all this, she's crazy when it comes to her home. It's her temple; she will not change a hair of it even though it means continuing to use the stairs. She tells me if I were a "good daughter" I would come over and do the things an aide does. I have always been a good daughter; in fact, I was never able to say no to her, but now I don't know what to do. I have a career which I love and need, two teenage children who need me, and a husband who is furious with me, because at the end of the day I have nothing left for him and the kids. All I do is talk about my mother, to my friends, to my relatives; she has become an obsession. If my mother falls and there is no one there to help her she'll fall again, maybe hurt herself more seriously this time, and it will be my fault.

She asks me, "Can you come to my mother's house to speak with her? Maybe she'll listen to you." How can I help this distressed daughter, who cares deeply about her mother and is committed to doing what's right for her, achieve some balance in her life? First, I explain to her (we'll call her Joan) that my coming to visit her mother as a total stranger and at *her* behest would antagonize Mother even more. I would, and understandably so, be perceived as the enemy by Mother. I suggest that Joan call Mother's doctor, with whom Mother already has a positive relationship, and ask him to intervene. His reading of the riot act to her just might cause her to yield. Second, and more important, what can be done about Joan's fear that Mother might fall again, but this time fatally so, and that she will be to blame? If Mother doesn't do what the doctor tells her to do and comes home without aides, will Joan, in order to be the dependable adult child she wishes to be, have to quit her job and take care of her mother? If her mother does fall again and if she doesn't quit her job, how will she be able to live with her guilt and selfishness?

In order to counsel Joan effectively, we must first explore her family history, of which she has already given us strong clues. The history of Joan's relationship with her mother is marked by a dominance-submission theme. Mother's relationship with her husband was apparently characterized by the same pattern. Joan was quite clear that her mother was a demanding, authoritarian figure, and even as a child it was hard to stand up to her without experiencing guilt and anxiety.

Old people can and do change if they want to, but generally a person's personality does not vary much through the years. Extensive research on later-life development has proven that as we age we become more of whatever we were when we were younger, so that the warm, giving person becomes warmer and more giving; the unfriendly, distancing person becomes more unfriendly and aloof. Although the potential to change any relationship exists if both parties to that relationship are willing, from what we know about personality patterns and old age, Joan's mother will not be motivated to do an about-face. Mother's long-standing personality is authoritarian in nature; she must be in control of the significant people in her life, in this case her daughter, and she must control her environment. She does not want additional help. She will not spoil the decor of her home, knowing full well that without these measures she risks falling again. Are we at a standstill then? Can anything be done to change this situation? If Mother will not change, what can Joan do? The answer is that Joan can do plenty. She is not in the helpless position she thinks she is in.

With certainty we know Joan cannot continue to care for her mother, her husband, and her children and function at her job all at the same time without burning out or becoming ill. She must learn to *set limits*, to realize and to accept there is only so much she can do for her mother. This is not an easy task for a daughter who is deeply invested in being a good daughter and whose concept of what a good daughter is rests on sacrificing her personal needs to her mother's. How can Joan sustain a feeling of self-worth, if in doing less for Mother she feels she has failed as a daughter?

She might begin her process of setting limits by taking the huge leap of communicating to her mother exactly what she feels. Perhaps she would say something like this:

> JOAN: "Mom, I know how much you want me to spend more time taking care of you. I would like to and feel bad that I can't. I love you and have always been a good daughter, but I have a husband and children who need me, as well as a job which I cannot give up. This is the way it has to be Mom, or I'll get sick myself. There are home-health aides out there, whom you can afford. I want to visit when I can, still take you out to lunch or to the doctor, make phone calls for you when necessary, but I can't do any more. I'll get sick if I do. And if I get sick then you won't have me to depend on for all the other things."
>
> MOM MAY REPLY: "But you know I don't want strangers in my house, going through my things and upsetting everything. You know this about me and you can still say what you are saying. There's no point in my living anymore if my one and only daughter doesn't care, if I have to depend on strangers."
>
> JOAN: "Look Mom, I do care and you know it. I won't say it again but I must take this stand. If I get sick I'll be of no help to anyone."

The above dialogue could be a beginning. It is a decision that Joan has to make and is a difficult one for a daughter who has always yielded to her mother. It may take weeks or even months for her to feel comfortable in this new role. She will need reinforcement from her husband and friends. She might even join a support group composed of other adult children who are experiencing the same difficulty. She may seek professional help from a clinical social worker or a psychologist.

Joan is not alone in her inability to set limits on caregiving to her mother. There are thousands upon thousands of other daughters and sons who feel they too should be doing more. Elaine Brody[6] posits the idea that adult children, someplace deep down, feel they must give the same total care to their aging parents that their parents gave to them as children. Although intellectually we know we cannot take care of our parents in such a complete manner, our hearts dictate to us that we can and our consciences that we should. Therefore, we continue to care, to do, and to give, feeling a gnawing guilt that we are not doing enough. Certainly we know that babies grow up and become independent while aging parents can only become more dependent and require more difficult personal care. All of this matters naught—the unconscious seems to rule, establishing unobtainable goals.

The "catch-22" of the guilt-producing process is that when we become angry over doing too much for our parent, we feel guilty because we tell ourselves it is wrong to harbor anger toward an elderly parent. As a result, we increase our caregiving efforts to atone for the forbidden anger we feel. As we redouble caregiving to prove we are "good children," the anger resurfaces producing the guilt we tried to get rid of in the first place. A client of mine who became angry with her father for an insensitive demand felt so guilty that the next day she not only granted him his request but also offered to do more. The "extra," which necessitated cancelling an important appointment for herself, threw her into further rage and guilt. The guilt-manufacturing apparatus that exhorts us to do more and more turns out and pours back into the machine the same raw materials to perpetuate the cycle. Destructive and unending, the anger-guilt-anger cycle eats away at the caregiver, causing stress in the form of depression, anxiety, or psychosomatic illness. Setting limits is a way to put a chink into this self-feeding, self-defeating machinery.

Caregivers often reassure me that they can manage their multitude of responsibilities by "juggling"; that, for example, a daughter can take her mother to the eye doctor on a given day by doing the following: one, taking the morning off from work; two, working late the next day to make up for the lost time; three, postponing her own doctor's appointment until next month when she is again allowed another half day. Juggling involves looking at your calendar and figuring out how much you can squeeze into a day or what you can cut out of one day and add to another. Only, juggling never quite works because there are not enough hours to accommodate increasing demands. The day does not expand to meet our ever growing, overwhelming responsibilities. We always end up short—rushed, tense, having less and less time to devote to activities we enjoy and value. The fact is that even the most skillful juggler can keep just so many balls in the air. When he exceeds his limits, the balls come crashing down. Only in the case of the caregiver the stakes are higher than an unsuccessful performance; they are his own physical and emotional health. Setting limits means eliminating some of the balls so that the caregiver can restore balance to his life.

The sixty-five-year-old daughter (whom we will call Rose) of phone call 2, who desperately needs to get away from her stressful caregiving situation but is afraid that separation from Mother might result in Mother's death, has also not learned to set limits. In this instance, we have a caregiver who is approaching old age herself. In addition to caring for her mother, she has been caring for an ailing spouse. Her recent retirement, eagerly anticipated as the beginning of an era of fun for her husband and her, never materializes as such. Now, born of necessity, not luxury, she makes the decision to go away. The decision, however, is not a clear, simple one; it is conflicted. She feels guilty and selfish about taking time for herself. She is anxious that her mother might die while she is gone as, indeed, her mother says she will.

When I see Rose in my office, I see a woman who is intelligent, sensitive, and decent, but exploding with rage. For six years, she tells me she has been a loyal, sacrificing daughter. After her father died and her mother moved in with her, she did everything possible to make Mother comfortable in her home, including taking her to movies, friends' homes, and dinners with her husband and her. When her mother was hospitalized with her stroke she visited every day. When her mother was at a rehab center, she did likewise. Then her husband became ill and she says she felt like a "double-duty nurse." She recognizes that she has been getting angrier and angrier, and at this point resents every bit of care she extends to her mother. She weeps, saying, "If I didn't feel so guilty I'd put her in a nursing home so my husband and I can finally live a little. Sometimes, I'm ashamed to say, I think I hate her."

Had Rose learned to set limits early on in her efforts to care for her mother, the entire situation might not have soared out of control. She and I talked for a long time about the intensity of her relationship with Mother. I learned she was the only child of a very dependent mother and hardworking father who was away from home most of the time on business. Rose felt she had always taken care of her mother; always filled a void created by her father's absence. In our sessions, she realized she never wanted children because she was burned out from taking care of her mother. "And here I am burned out again," she would say, "but with no father to at least share some of the burden with me. Before I know it, I'll be old and my life will be over."

With help, Rose was able to tell her mother how she felt and that she and her husband were going away. Since money was not a problem, she told Mother she would provide the best live-in help and even call her twice while she was gone. Her mother, of course, was furious, accusing her of cruel abandonment and complete selfishness. But Rose remained firm, went away with her husband, had a wonderful time, and her mother survived.

When she returned we met individually a few more times and then she joined my support group. Through the support of the group, she eventually came to the sad realization that she would have to put her mother in a nursing home. Her husband's health was not improving and she herself was becoming increasingly depressed and tired. She knew it would destroy her to continue to care for her mother in the same complete manner. Of course, she continued to experience guilt. In time, however, she learned that she could still be a good daughter while doing less for her mother. With more time now for herself and her husband, she became less angry. As a result, when she made nursing home visits to her mother, these visits became less stressful and more meaningful.

How truly sad it is that for many adult sons and daughters like Rose, "To honor thy Father and Mother" means they have no right to honor themselves—which of course is what setting limits is all about. Setting limits entails the recognition and acceptance of what you can and cannot realistically do for your parents and then communicating this information to your parents in an empathic and sensitive manner. Setting limits is not an act of selfishness, but one of caring for your parents as well as for yourself. More often than not, your parents, to your surprise, will accommodate your needs. Parents do not want to be alienated from their children; they want and need to be wanted and loved by them. And when limits are set by adult children, not from anger but from a mature stance based on knowing their strengths and limitations, parents will usually respond positively.

Setting limits also means not sacrificing personally fulfilling activities and pursuits to caregiving chores. Indeed, you will be a more patient and empathic caregiver by continuing to do the things you love. Emotional replenishment is essential to compensate for the large quantities of energy expended in the myriad of concrete and emotional tasks inherent in the caregiving process. The optimal sources for such reenergizing are those pursuits that give us pleasure. Whether it is playing tennis or bridge or watching soap operas, the surrender of leisure activities will inevitably make us angry and resentful. Respite from caregiving is a must, else we dread each morning with the knowledge that there is nothing enjoyable in store for us. It takes conscious and deliberate effort on the part of the caregiver to make sure that he continues to enjoy those activities he enjoyed before his parents' dependencies intruded upon his lifestyle. Adult children who do not plan structured time for themselves report depression, moodiness, sleeplessness, increased anxiety, and a kind of "weltschmertz," described by one adult daughter as feeling "as if my life has lost all meaning and purpose."

Indeed, a person's identity can be negated as she immerses herself into her parents' needs, thoughts, and multiple crises. With days defined in terms of doctors' appointments, meal preparation, rehab exercises, and repeated explanations of routines and medications to assorted home-health aides, the caregiver feels drowned in a sea of endless ministrations, which do nothing to validate that she too is a person with needs and feelings. Consequently, it is truly a matter of health or sickness that we set aside time for an outing with friends or an evening at the movies or a few hours with the telephone off the hook just to do as we wish. For those caregivers whose parents live with them, the continued pursuit of outside interests becomes even more imperative. Such persons must make it their business to get away on a regular basis in order to prevent the kind of stress that can lead to hurtful behavior, either to themselves in the form of alcohol or drug misuse, or to their parent in the form of neglect or abuse.

I alluded to "granny bashing" in the introduction to this book. Suffice it to say that allowing ourselves to care for ourselves by doing things we enjoy, and not sacrificing pleasurable activities to caregiving chores, is the best insurance against this dreaded happening. It is important to remember that we are human beings with definable limits. Even the most giving, gentlest people, when taxed beyond endurance, could resort to harmful acting out. We are all vulnerable when the circumstances become unmanageable. The problem is that we do not pay heed to the inner distress signals: the gritting of teeth, the knots in the stomach, the increased irritability over meaningless peccadilloes, the headaches and backaches. These symptoms indicate that we are no longer coping and that it is time to change whatever it is that we are doing.

"But I cannot leave Mother or Dad alone," you say. If this is the case, then hire someone to sit. If you cannot afford to do this, then ask a neighbor or friend and return her kindness with a favor of your own. A caregiver I know takes care of her neighbor's six-year-old son after school in exchange for that neighbor's "mother-sitting" services two nights each week. If brothers and sisters live nearby, try to involve them. As I mention in chapter 6, if siblings have been reluctant to do their share, tell them honestly how you are feeling. Tell them you are exhausted and burned out and that unless they pitch in, you will get sick. A direct and assertive communication about your circumstances may often bring an uninvolved brother or sister back into the picture.

Many times a parent does not mind being left alone. The fear and panic emanate from the adult child. Therefore, ask your parent how he would feel if you had an afternoon or evening off. If your parent says he would mind, tell him you absolutely must get out or you will be of no use either to him or yourself. Leave a friend's telephone number to call if he becomes anxious. If this is not possible, CONTACT, the telephone reassurance answering service, is always available. Find out as well which hospitals offer medic alert systems, so that all your parent has to do when he needs emergency help is push a button located on a disk worn around his neck.

If your parent lives with you and you desperately need a vacation but have no one to care for Mother or Father, then look into respite care. Respite care services consist of temporary in-facility twenty-four-hour supervision for persons who depend upon a primary caregiver for support. Nursing homes, hospitals, and rehab centers are the usual sites for this type of care and allow from fifteen to thirty live-in days. Some programs are state subsidized, so that families with low to moderate incomes and assets can avail themselves of these vital services on a co-pay basis.

With respite care, the adult child can take a break for a few days to a few weeks, knowing that her parent will receive competent personal and medical supervision and care. Information on respite care is available through your local area Office on Aging or local hospital. Just a weekend away from caregiving chores can make a considerable difference in the caregiver's attitude and disposition. Remember, caregiving is work—stressful and all-consuming. As with any job, one must occasionally take a breather in order to maintain motivation. The penalty for this kind of self-neglect is burn-out, culminating in physical or emotional illness.

Keep in mind that adult children whose parents live with them are more vulnerable to stress-related illness (for example, headaches, backaches, or stomach disorders) than other caregivers. An excellent example of the powerful effect of emotions on the body was provided by a dermatologist friend. He told me that among his female patients suffering from neurodermatitis (a stress-related eczema characterized by itching, redness, and inflammation) it was not uncommon to see flare-ups in daughters whose mothers moved back in with them. Unlike Asia or Europe where generations have traditionally lived with one another, in our society the combination of adult child and elderly parent under the same roof can create unbearable tension. Unless both generations have practiced this living arrangement for a lifetime, it rarely works.

Take care of yourselves! Eat well, get enough sleep, and push yourself to exercise. A fifteen-minute walk every day can make an enormous difference in your mood and attitude. Rent a movie that will make you laugh and laugh and laugh some more. Norman Cousins, in his uplifting book, *Anatomy of an Illness*,[7] has proven to us that laughter is the magic potion to heal ailing minds and bodies.

Remember, the effectiveness of your caregiving is in direct proportion to its quality. The underpinning of quality care cannot be anger, guilt, or resentment. Setting limits keeps these negative and destructive emotions at bay.

Over the years, however, I have been struck by how much more difficult it is for daughters than for sons to set limits. As a result, caregiving is a more stressful experience for them than for their male counterparts. In an effort to be "good daughters," they place their needs secondary to those of their parents. No matter how outrageous a parent's demand in terms of what the daughter can and cannot give of her time, energy, and health, she cannot say no. There is no question in my mind that our inability to say no grows out of the socialization of women to please others. We have been taught to believe that to fill the expectations of significant people (parents, husband, children) in our lives is a prime requisite to being a lovable and worthwhile female. To use a term coined by sociologist David Riesman[8] in another context many years ago, women are truly "other directed" human beings, in that how they feel about themselves is based upon how others feel about them. Men, on the other hand, are more "inner directed." As a result, men are able to be assertive in their key relationships without experiencing anxiety over not being liked.

Nowhere has this disparity between men and women shown itself more clearly than in the composition of my support groups. Members of my groups are always daughters. I do receive phone calls from sons, who tell me about their parents and ask a lot of questions about support groups, but counseling efforts are limited to those conversations. Often sons tell me that perhaps a sister or wife might come to a meeting. Moreover, the note of desperation, bell clear in the voice of a daughter caller, is conspicuously absent from the son's queries. Not agonizing over whether they should be doing more or excoriating themselves with guilt, sons generally seem to have a more laid-back attitude toward caregiving. (See chapter 10 for more about differences in gender.)

A highly intelligent, sensitive forty-nine-year-old daughter in one of my support groups poignantly told the group how impossible it is for her to say no to her mother. A working mother herself, she had given up valuable leisure time for her mother and neglected other family members. Indeed, the caregiving situation had gotten so out of hand that her daughter openly admitted to hating her grandmother for taking her mother away from her so much. One day when this daughter felt she was actually becoming sick from all the pressures, she telephoned her brother, who lived three hundred miles away, and asked him to take Mother for a week. During this visit her brother firmly told Mother that he and his wife would do the best they could to provide her with an enjoyable time, but that he would not cater to any of her "ridiculous" demands. He additionally informed his mother that his family came first. By the time Mother's little visit ended, she knew she would never return to Brother's home. When Daughter later spoke to her brother about what had happened she was shocked by his matter-of-fact attitude. She reported to the group: "He sounded as if 'well, what other way is there for me to behave?'" She found it unbelievable that her brother could stand up to their mother without experiencing the anxiety and guilt that would have torn her to pieces. She told us she wished she could behave likewise. She stated that unlike her, her brother would not allow their mother to destroy his life.

This daughter, Joan, and Rose are part of a large group of women, caring and decent, who are caught in a Mother-Daughter pattern that is difficult to change. The submission to a strong self-absorbed mother, which begins in early childhood, intensifies when that mother reaches old age and the daughter reaches middle age. The demands that Mother makes upon Daughter at this turning point cause more anger and resentment than at any previous times in the life cycle. Because the caregiving experience acts as a catalyst to bring old suppressed emotions to the surface, this crisis offers an opportunity to adult daughters to do some soul searching and to make changes. Believe me, although your mothers may not be able to change, you can. And *your* change may bring a positive change to your relationship with your mother. If the adult child can learn to accept that which cannot be changed or to express her needs and feelings to her parent with confidence, not guilt, then the ripple effect of her newly acquired maturity alters the whole parent-child relationship.

A good friend, sixty-five, single, and retired from a successful career in teaching, who has been living amicably with her eighty-seven-year-old mother off and on for thirty-five years, said to me: "Tell them, Viv, it takes maturity to make the caregiving experience work. It's as simple as all that and I really don't see what all the fuss is about." Of course, my friend is right. It does take maturity. The rub is most of us are not so lucky to have mature parents or to be so fully grown up ourselves. In my friend's case, the relationship is beautifully balanced, with each mature enough to accept the other as a separate individual with different needs requiring respect. The mold for my friend's mature relationship with her mother was cast before they became "elderly parent–adult child." Their patterns of interactions, the raw materials of which the mold was made, have not altered significantly throughout the years.

My friend's favored circumstances, however, are the exception. Those who come to me for help are representative of the more common caregiving dilemmas. They view the aging of their parents and the caregiving experience as a final opportunity to become mature—a separate, whole person who can act independently of a parent's approval or disapproval. (More on this subject is presented in chapter 8, "Seeing Our Parents as People.") They are aware of how hard it is to change old behavioral patterns toward a parent, but they are motivated and determined to try. Willing to test new strategies, to take a fresh look at their role in their relationship with Mother or Dad, and to examine feelings previously suppressed, they are able to effect results. They are shocked and pleased when their newly earned maturity has made a positive impact, for example, upon a rigid, authoritarian parent. "Yes, you're right." "I have been selfish and didn't realize it." "I don't like what you have to say, but you have a point." "I can now see your side of the picture." Responses such as these come from parents after an adult child has confidently confronted them with an unfair demand or an outright manipulation. The relationship changes as each interacts with the other on a new level, as separate people with differing needs, which each party respects. What if the total relationship does not change, but you have? Then what? Your own personal growth and new ability to set limits confidently are well worth your efforts.

As I write this, I cannot help but wonder and hope that things will be different for our daughters and us when we reach this watershed. Our daughters, after all, have been socialized to be independent; to seek self-worth within themselves and not from others. Likewise, from our own experiences caring for our mothers, we have become sensitive to the special needs of our daughters during middle age and know how eroding endless demands can be to a relationship. I am confident that we and our daughters, as a result of increased inner awareness and knowledge, will respond to the caregiving challenge in a healthier, more mutually satisfying manner.

A word of caution about the expression "setting limits" is necessary before the close of this chapter. Inasmuch as the concept of setting limits is also used by those who teach parent effectiveness, confusion about the use of the term in the context of elder care may exist. As part of parent effectiveness training, young parents are taught to set limits on their children as a means to teach discipline. As distinct from child care, in elder care, limits are set by adult children on themselves, not on their parents. Some who falsely believe old age is a regression to childhood may misrepresent setting limits as a validation of role reversal. Much more will be written about role reversal in chapter 5. It is important here, however, to be clear that setting limits refers only to setting limits upon ourselves as caregivers. Setting limits is a mature act that enables us to take care of ourselves and to give care to our parents without resentment.

4

Unrealistic Expectations

I T is impossible to set limits if our expectations of what we think we can and should do for our parents are unrealistic. Of course, what is realistic for one adult child may not be for another. For example, the adult daughter who is not working, has grown children who are independent and a husband who is not resentful when she tends to her mother's needs, may and can realistically expect more from herself than her counterpart who is saddled with a set of reverse conditions. Each caregiver is unique in terms of personality, capacity to nurture or to give care, present and past family history, and social and economic circumstances. Consequently, it is not fair that all caregivers should be expected to give the same quality and quantity of care to their elderly parents. There are general guidelines, however, gleaned from years of listening to the conflicts and difficulties experienced by adult children, that I believe can be helpful in determining realistic expectations for ourselves within the caregiving context. These guidelines will serve as boundaries in which to set limits. Besides, we have just so much psychic and physical energy; knowing where not to squander it can only be beneficial.

In any relationship, from marriage to employer-employee, it takes two committed people to make it work. The relationship between aging parent and grown child is no exception. The adult child who is emotionally ready to be a dependable caregiver to his parent, but finds that his parent is not willing to be dependent upon him, is stuck. For some parents, to accept dependency upon their children for anything means the end of their important lifelong role as a parent. With all the losses they have had to endure and over which they could exert no control, to remain parents to their grown children becomes, in a sense, the final holdout against surrender of total identity. Unlike the parents described in chapter 2, who resist help to maintain a realistic level of independence, these parents, in their tenacity to cling to the parental role, often prevent their adult children from giving them necessary care.

The complaint from adult children caught in this morass may typically sound like this: "My mother is stubborn. She will not allow me to come in and help with the cooking or laundry, nor will she allow anyone else to come to help. She has severe arthritis and fluid buildup in her ankles, some days she can hardly walk, but she insists on doing everything herself. I am so angry I could kill her! I know she's going to fall and break a hip." Or, "My mother refuses to go to the doctor. I keep after her but she will not listen. And the more I push her the more she resists. What should I do?" For parents such as these, the only means left to exercise control over their environment is to remain a parent to their children at all costs. As long as they have the sense that they can still tell their children what to do, life has meaning and purpose—all is not lost. As matriarchs-in-chief, issuing commands to their children, they are able to receive emotional gratification from an environment that has little to offer them as the years slip by.

What course can the adult child take in this instance? The answer seems to lie in acceptance of the situation for what it is—for example, a way for a parent to achieve some mastery over her fate. We cannot expect, after so many years and at this time of life, that some of our parents will give up that which is so vital to their self-worth. Our parent's old age and our middle age are not appropriate periods in which to engage in an adolescent struggle for power. There is no comfort for either side in such a contest. To understand the basis for such resistance from parents enables the adult child to establish more realistic expectations for the relationship. Such insight, additionally, relieves the pain of rejection we experience when our parents won't let us be dependable and prevents us from falsely personalizing or perceiving our parent's destructive behavior as our fault or our responsibility.

Another practical and benign strategy, when you know the source of your parent's resistance to help is her unwillingness to surrender the parental role, is to say something like this: "Mom, I'm really sorry you won't accept my help. You are still boss, and whenever you are ready for me to help out, just let me know and I'll be there. In the meantime, if you feel there's something else I can do just let me know." In making such a statement to your parent, you not only offer her a choice, but also allow her to remain a parent in full control of what she wishes of you, her adult child. Your stance has prevented an embroilment that would leave both participants angry and resentful.

But, you ask, "Aren't there risks in allowing our parents to act in such ways? They can really hurt themselves if we don't at times actively intervene." Yes, of course there are risks. And do not think for a minute that your parents are not aware of them. But old people must be allowed to take those risks that are vital to their sense of mastery and self-worth. The son in chapter 2, who returned the car keys to his mother, is an example of an adult child who permitted a parent to take such a necessary risk. Certainly, risks have to be weighed. If, for example, the mother in chapter 2 had been disoriented and confused to the point of being a danger to herself and others, then the son would have shown poor judgment in allowing her to drive. The daughter, described at the beginning of this chapter, who won't give up badgering her mother to get help for fear her mother will fall and break her hip, has to let go. Her mother may, indeed, fall and break her hip but her daughter must risk this disaster.

We can fill some of our parents' needs easily and without too much distress to ourselves. Others we cannot, and yet we unrealistically expect that we should. Perhaps the greatest loss experienced by aging parents is the loss of friends with whom so much meaningful time has been shared throughout the years. As a result of this depletion of contemporaries, our parents suffer deep voids of loneliness. Many adult children feel they can and should fill these gaps. In a recent telephone conversation with a caring adult son, he told me how disappointed his parents are that he and his wife cannot spend just about every weekend with them. It seems his parents recently moved to their state in order to be near their children and grandchildren. As the son put it, "My parents moved ten years too late. My children are teenagers, living their own lives, one of them even began college this year. I'm torn when they voice their disappointment to me, but I feel I must live my own life and my parents, though in their late seventies, are healthy and vital enough to live theirs." And so be it! It is impossible for adult children to compensate for the camaraderie and intimacy that only years of close friendship can achieve. We cannot replace our parents' friends and confidants. The adult child who expects this of himself not only establishes unrealistic goals but also sets himself up for failure which, as we have learned, results in resentment and subsequent guilt.

Most elderly people are depressed (see chapter 15). The painful and successive losses experienced by the old person render it impossible to feel otherwise. With loss of job, loss of friends and spouse, and increased frailty and decline in physical and mental function, the old person will feel a sadness, a melancholy, a despair over her shrinking world. Some old persons, in spite of enormous physical and emotional trials, are able to keep depression at bay. Some experience it only minimally. Some, however, are overcome by it; they spend whatever time is left to them withdrawn, socially isolated, and absorbed in endless negative ruminations about their unfulfilled pasts. Some lie immobile in beds or sit in the same chairs day after day. The history and personality of the old person will pretty much determine whether he will succumb to or survive depression.

Many an adult child has come to me with deep concern over a parent's depression. The opening remarks of one adult daughter went like this: "My mother is seventy, really quite young. She retired three years ago and my father died a year later. She lives in her own apartment, manages to care for it and herself pretty well, but she won't go out and seems no longer to have a zest for living. I have put her in touch with senior groups, but she says the people in them are all too old for her. My husband and I take her out all the time. I really try to entertain her, but nothing helps. I feel so bad for her. I feel I should be doing more for her. What else can I do?"

Upon closer questioning of the daughter, I learned that her mother had been very dependent upon her husband for social and emotional comforts. I additionally learned that Mother had always been anxious about reaching out to others and that her basic outlook on life was, as long as Daughter could remember, gloomy and negative. Now her husband was gone, as was her job, which provided some structure and social contact. This mother's personality, dependent and pessimistic, diminished her ability to cope with her current losses. As a result, she became depressed.

This daughter unrealistically believed she should and could

"cure" her mother's depression. She thought that if she kept her busy and entertained her, Mother would be all right. After a few counseling sessions, she recognized that she did not have it within her power to rescue Mother; that she was emotionally draining herself in thinking that she could. Mother's cure would have to come from within her, and given Mother's history, this was unlikely without professional help. Daughter could, however, continue to plan family events, which would give Mother something to look forward to. These outings, though, should take place when Daughter has time and energy. The kind of constant, frenzied recreational activities Daughter had provided were unproductive to Mother as far as curing her and were burning out Daughter. I, furthermore, suggested to Daughter that she make an effort to convince her mother to see a gero-psychiatrist for antidepressant medications. There are several such drugs on the market that work wonders on old people's depression. Psychiatrists, knowledgeable in geriatric pharmacology, know just which ones to prescribe. Counseling, of course, was also recommended. Although Daughter would suggest both these essential treatments to Mother, Daughter's increased understanding of Mother's depression prepared her for the negative response she received. Of more importance was Daughter's newly found ability to react to Mother's rejection of help not as a cry for immediate rescue of Mother but, realistically, as Mother's painful problem that Mother herself must conquer.

Because we unrealistically expect ourselves never to lose patience with a parent, we feel deep remorse whenever we do. We cannot, however, always be composed when faced with some of a parent's behaviors. When adult child and parent live with each other, tensions can run especially high. With parent and caregiver thrown together daily, the odds for generational collision increase. A daughter may bristle at her mother's invasions into her kitchen and privacy: "She's always looking over my shoulder to check if I've put enough salt into the soup"; or "she wants to talk when all I want is to be left alone after a day at work." Even when parent and child do not live under the same roof, a parent's anxious repetitions, continuing commentaries on the state of her health, or slowness of movements can cause utter exasperation. We snap, act testy, and feel guilt and regret afterward. We cannot forgive ourselves for our lack of compassion and respect. These outbursts go with the territory of caregiving. So forgive yourself, tell your parent how genuinely sorry you are, and be less hard on yourself the next time it happens.

Although I have emphasized over and over again the importance of giving care willingly rather than from guilt or anger, I must caution that it is unrealistic and absurd to expect that we will always be able to minister to our parents' needs with a glowing smile. There will be many times when these darker emotions are the source of our care, and this is okay. Our elderly parents' multiple problems and dependencies spawn so many crises and emergencies that it is impossible to have complete control over the caregiving situation. We cannot foresee what tomorrow will bring to our parents' tenuous daily lives. There will be occasions when we must punch our pillows, stamp our feet, perhaps cry from helplessness and frustration, knowing full well that there is no way we can turn our backs on our parents' call for help.

An adult daughter, a dependable caregiver to her mother in every sense, whose vacation unexpectedly coincided with her mother's first two weeks in a nursing home, told me through bitter tears: "I had to cancel my trip. There was no way I could not be with my mother during this crucial period without feeling like the most selfish person in the world. If she had already been in the home, it would have been different; I could have left without feeling guilty. But in this instance, how can I? I could kill her for her poor timing! I just hope I have enough self-control not to show her what I am feeling."

A less dramatic example may be the son who receives a call from Dad just as he is about to go out the door to play tennis. Dad tells him that the aide who usually comes to bathe him and put him to bed cannot make it because her car has broken down. Could he come over for "just a little bit" to help him through these rituals? As much as he hates to give up his pleasurable evening and as enraged as he may be over Dad's demand at this inopportune moment, he knows he must go to him. He would feel incredibly guilty if he left Dad in the lurch, and under such circumstances, guilt is what he should feel. After all, such calls from Dad are rare, and to reject him in this way would be self-serving.

And how about those times when we're just plain tired—from work, from family, from everything. We would just like to be alone, to sleep, to read, to watch T.V., perhaps to do nothing. Of course, we are angry when that call comes and we know we must be there for our parents. It is perfectly acceptable to feel anger and to continue to feel it as we do what we must do for our parents.

The infrequent instances that dictate that we give care from resentment or guilt present no problem. We cannot have control over every facet of our parents' lives, even if we live under the same roof with them. Nor should we strive for this outcome. The irrationality and destructiveness of such a goal is what this book is about. Furthermore, as noted in chapter 2, the majority of our parents do not want us to serve as "watchmen" over their daily doings. To carry filial responsibility to such extremes renders our parents helpless and robs them of the right to determine their own destiny for as long as they are able. It destroys their essential dignity, without which life is not worth living. Therefore, we must not be hard on ourselves on those occasions when we cannot set limits, and consequently find that we are becoming angry in the process of helping our parents. We cannot be all-knowing and all-present; things will happen to upset well-laid plans and it is all right to be angry and resentful at such times.

Care given continuously and over a long period of time from anger and resentment paints quite a different picture. It sets into motion the "anger, guilt, more I must do" cycle that burns out the caregiver and transforms the very nature of what care is and how it should be given. It makes care a heavy chore, stripped of the gratification it can bring to both donor and donee.

Care, upon occasion, even in the closest, most loving family, may be extended to parents from obligation. This is healthy and acceptable. The circumstances that give rise to care from obligation may be similar to some of those mentioned above; only the darker emotions of anger and guilt are missing. Care from obligation is care from duty; it is given not because we really want to, but because we feel we must because it is the right and proper thing to do. Care given from obligation can emanate from love as well as intense dislike. An adult son, in a most matter-of-fact manner, said to me: "I never really liked my mother that much, but I did what I felt I should and never felt guilt after she died." On the other hand, when we are close to a parent, we may find it especially hard to differentiate between obligation and love. The line can be fuzzy; the feelings, the ingredients that comprise care from obligation are elusive and difficult to identify.

The sense that I was giving care to my dad from obligation occurred when he asked me if, on my day off, I would travel over one hundred miles to take him to visit one of his few remaining relatives, who although meant nothing to me meant everything to him. Did I want to do this? No, but of course I took him. How could I refuse to honor the request of this sweet man who had given me so much? Was this love or obligation? That I deeply love my father lent a certain grace to my act, but there is no doubt in my mind that the central force that motivated me was obligation.

The point is that tending to our parents' needs from obligation is inherent in the caregiving process. It is not unhealthy or unnatural. To the contrary, it is a human response for which we should not judge ourselves harshly. As caregivers, it is essential that we understand the complexities and facets of every kind of care. Without this knowledge, we cannot be realistic in our expectations and our goals.

Although I have described reminiscence (see chapter 5) in old people as healthy behavior, there is a kind of reminiscence that is negative and destructive to the elderly person. During a lunchtime workshop I conducted, a bright young woman asked me how she could handle her grandmother, who was always reminiscing about what a terrible, unhappy life she had lived. This young woman told me that she sits listening to her grandmother for hours trying to get her to sing a less sad song. She said her efforts are always fruitless and she leaves her grandmother's side as frustrated and depressed as her grandmother. I told her there is really little she can do about this. She certainly cannot change her grandmother's past, which, as was the case, was filled with hardship and deprivation. Nor can she miraculously transform her grandmother's inability to find and focus upon some of the pleasurable things in her life. The more she spoke about her grandmother's personality, the more she realized her grandmother had always had a rather negative attitude toward life, and that as she aged this attitude became more hardened. As a solution, I suggested that she see her grandmother less frequently and for shorter time periods. There was no point in making herself miserable too, and she might have more control over the content of Grandmother's conversation during limited visitations. The end result was her recognition that she could no longer realistically expect that her intensive efforts would change her grandmother's lifelong personality, which was at the root of her unhealthy reminiscence.

We must let go of our unrealistic expectations that we can be all and do all for our parents. We cannot be dependable caregivers to our parents if they will not allow us. We cannot fill the emptiness in our parents' lives that results from the loss of valued friends and family. We cannot always give care from love, strength, and charity. We can neither cure our parents' depressions nor compensate for their past regrets and hardships. We cannot foresee and protect our parents from every risk. We cannot always practice patience and forbearance. To accept all that we cannot do is painful and sad; yet it is an essential condition to giving our parents the kind of care we can take pride in now and when they are no longer with us.

5

Role Reversal

"IT's the role reversal part that is so tough for me. You know, I see my dad becoming a child again. I have to cut up his food and help him dress. And half the time, believe it or not, he has the look of a child on his face. I find myself even treating him like a baby, which somehow doesn't feel right. I just can't handle all this, really. It's terrifying and also makes me enraged." These words were spoken to me by an anguished, sensitive fifty-eight-year-old son who was primary caregiver to his eighty-year-old father. This son and I spent several counseling sessions together talking about the concept of role reversal. An extremely bright man, eminent in his profession of civil engineering, he had always been under the impression that as people age they become children again who must in turn now be parented by their grown children. He had a clear role model for this kind of caregiving behavior, because he remembered his mother treating his elderly grandfather, who had lived with them, in a baby-like manner. He spoke of how his mother would change her voice—condescending, "as a nurse would speak to her hospitalized patient"—when addressing him, and how she wouldn't even let him, over protests that he was able, button his own sweater. He loved his grandfather very much and the uncomfortable feeling that his mother was in some way destroying her father's pride and spirit remained with him to the present time, when he found himself in the same caregiving position. He was trying to replicate his mother's behavior, but ancient voices from his childhood were telling him, "this is the wrong way to treat Dad." Those voices were telling him right.

The definition of role reversal that governed my client's caregiving to his father is held by many. It is a false definition, which must be corrected if we are to minister to our elderly parents' needs with sensitivity, respect, and love. No matter how old and frail or mentally confused your parent may be, he is still your parent. When my fifty-eight-year-old friend visits her mother, who has Alzheimer's, in the nursing home, there is nothing condescending in manner or voice when she shows her mother the new clothing she has bought her. Knowing how much her mother valued an attractive appearance in better days, she says with sincerity and genuine warmth, "I hope you like these new dresses, Mom. I know you prefer loose waistlines and V-necks." When she addresses her mother, she neither uses baby talk nor the first person plural "we." All communication is in terms of "I" and "you." For example: "How are *you*, Mom? *I* am fine." Similarly, a fifty-three-year-old son, who practiced law with his father for fifteen years, told me that when he visits his confused and disoriented father, he talks to him as if "Dad were still able to help me solve problems and encourage me when I feel down about losing a case."

Old age does not mean that our parent is placed in a Wells-like time machine, which hurls her back to someplace in childhood. Alex Comfort,[9] in his book on geriatric psychiatry, wisely notes that when he evaluates a family where he observes the children speaking to their elderly parents in an infantilizing manner, he knows that something is awry between the generations. All is not well in such families. Respect is lacking and angry feelings lurk behind the honey-smooth tones of adult children's voices.

Role reversal, then, does not mean that in old age our parents become children whom we parent. Role reversal, used correctly, refers to the turning point in the family when adult children become dependable caregivers to their parents. This does not mean that adult children become their parents' parents. To be dependable means to be there for our parents when they need us—not only for that ride to the doctor but also to lend an empathic ear, to listen.

It is said pejoratively by those who feel adult children are letting their parents down that "how come one mother can take care of ten children and ten children cannot take care of one mother?" The smugness of those who cite this catchphrase as undeniable proof of the adult child's failure to assume filial responsibility never ceases to throw me into complete rage. Of course it takes ten children to care for one elderly mother! Differences between caring for children and caring for elderly parents abound, and those differences must be explored in order to put to rest once and for all the glib and erroneous use of the "one mother-ten children" expression. A child is an unformed human being with no long historical relationship between her parent and her. She is molded by her parents from day one to fit into their lives in a certain way. She eats, plays, sleeps, and behaves for many years as they teach her, on their terms. Even an ornery three-year-old who protests going to the doctor can be persuaded by her parents to do so without causing them too much upset or stress. For example, she can be picked up bodily and placed in the car seat of her parent's automobile from which she can be carried, screaming, into the doctor's office. She can be promised a special treat if she cooperates or punished by withholding the same treat if she does not. Or she can be held and comforted by her parent throughout the entire ordeal. The point is that she can be coerced to do what is best for her. The imposition of these limits on a child is part and parcel of child rearing. It is not, however, one of the ingredients in appropriate and empathic elder care. Again, we set limits on ourselves, not on our parents. Imagine using these same techniques with your seventy-seven-year-old mother who desperately needs to see her physician but refuses to go. Can you pick her up bodily and place her in your automobile? Can you tell her there will be no ice cream cone if she is uncooperative and one if she accedes to your wishes? Can you just hug and stroke her with the reassuring words that "all will be okay"? Of course not! Issues of respect, acceptance of a parent's rights, and the physical realities and limitations of the adult body debilitated by the weaknesses of old age profoundly alter the picture.

Not too long ago, I took my three-year-old grandson on an outing. First, we went to a local mall to do some shopping, then we had lunch at a fast-food restaurant, followed by a trip to the park to feed the animals. I had a wonderful time. He was a delight and when I returned home, after dropping him off at his mother's, I felt absolutely exhilarated from the happy events of the day. I could not help contrast that day with one several years earlier when I took my eighty-two-year-old mother on a similar excursion. We also went shopping and out to lunch. Because I knew how difficult it was for my mother to be on time and appreciated that she did not want assistance from me with personal care, I would deliberately arrive at her apartment at least fifteen minutes late. She liked to be ready and waiting for me and if all went well, she was. If there was some snag in her morning routine and she could not be on time, she would be apologetic and deeply anxious (in spite of my reassurance that there was no need to rush) about upsetting my schedule. With her halting gait and poor balance, it would take us almost five minutes to maneuver the thirty yards, replete with seven steps, to my car. This slow pace would remain unchanged throughout the day. Further patience and restraint would be required from me in the shopping process itself. Respecting my mother's strong wish to be independent, I would merely stand by as she painstakingly got in and out of her garments to try on clothes, not allowing me to assist her with anything, save perhaps a difficult button on the sleeve.

Although I would grit my teeth in exasperation and anger, I could not help but admire her courage and tenacity. That I loved my mother and her company were not enough to stave off the complete exhaustion I would experience at the end of our sojourn together. The strain of constant vigilance combined with the slowing down of my normal rhythm to remain in sync with hers would wipe me out. With my three-year-old grandson, whenever he would tire or become moody, I could always put him in his stroller and off we'd go. My mother in a wheelchair! Never! Not that it would even have been inappropriate, given her advanced Parkinson's and later a broken hip. The fact is, she would not have allowed it and there was no way I could do other than respect her wish.

Our parents are not babies; we do not become their parents in a process of role reversal. The idea that ministering to an incontinent eighty-year-old is the same as changing the diapers of an eight-month-old is ludicrous. Madeleine L'Engle, in her moving book, *The Summer of the Great-Grandmother*, states it best when she contrasts the care given to her toddler daughter with that given to her eighty-seven-year-old mother:[10]

Old age has been compared to being once again like a baby: it is called second childhood. It is not. It is something very different. Charlotte is not yet two and not yet completely toilet trained. Her soiled diapers have the still-innocuous odor of a baby's. As we grow older, we as well as our environment, become polluted. The smell of both urine and feces becomes yearly stronger.

Although we all know that if we live long enough we run the risk of losing control over our bowels and bladder, our response to this reality is not benign acceptance. Rather, we cringe in shame and disgust. The word *incontinent*, as L'Engle points out, is a hard one to utter. It is not used when referring to a baby's pretoilet trained stage; interestingly enough, there is no single word for it in this context. If there were, with certainty, it would not carry the same implication of humiliation as incontinent.

The stamina and health of the caregiving adult child are other factors to be considered in the examination of role reversal and the "one mother-ten children" shibboleth. Young children have young parents. Young parents have boundless energy and both husband and wife are united in their enthusiasm to raise their children to adulthood. Though a young father-husband may harbor some feelings of resentment or alienation after the birth of a child, the issue of "who comes first" (see chapter 10) is short-lived. In a natural way, babies themselves elicit from us special nurturing juices, which are not called forth in caring for an elderly parent. Babies energize us to "koochie-koo" and cuddle them. We run to babies in supermarkets, at parties, and on the street to fuss over them. How often do we respond so joyously to an old person? Let's face it, caring for a baby can be just plain fun. Caring for an elderly parent rarely is. Caring for a baby can be stressful too, but there is a light at the end of the tunnel, because babies do grow up. And until they do, the developmental stages change rapidly enough to bring anticipation and delight to the caregiving experience. Elderly parents die, but sadly, until they do, they can be stuck in an unrelenting pattern of illness and depression that brings little comfort to the caregiver. Caregiving to the elderly has its deep and meaningful rewards, but they accrue only if the source of care is the joy of giving, not duty.

Adult children need lots of help in caring for their elderly parents. One adult daughter, unless she has neither family, job, nor other interests to pursue, is not sufficient to give quality care to her elderly mother. Such a scenario in the late twentieth century is doubtful. Adult children today have multiple responsibilities and demands and must marshal all the support they can—from siblings and other family members to community resources—in order to care adequately for an elderly parent. Our elderly parents are not babies, unformed, to fit into our lives and schedules as we wish. Issues of respect and history of relationship patterns determine our filial interactions. Nor are we, their caregivers, as young as we were when we raised our own children. One might appropriately ask what kind of care the mother of ten can give her children without the help of older siblings, baby-sitters, day-care centers, and grandparents. And when that mother of ten reaches old age, even if she is fortunate enough to have all her children near her and willing to care (which is unlikely; see chapter 6), she will still require additional help in order to get the quality care she deserves.

Parents, for as long as they live, do indeed remain parents to their children. Parents worry, fret, and give advice to their children though those children may be in their sixties. My mother, at age eighty-five, was still telling me not to walk around barefoot so much and worrying that I might get sick from working too hard. Whenever my husband and I would go away on vacation, both my parents had to know the exact time the plane would land and approximately when we thought we would actually be arriving at our house. Armed with this knowledge, they could benevolently exert their parental authority.

Perhaps the best example of the dictum, "your parent remains your parent no matter what his physical or mental condition," occurred during a support group meeting, when one of the members was describing the behavior of her confused and disoriented mother. The mother, recently widowed, quite depressed, and suffering brain damage as a result of several small strokes, would call her daughter "Mom" whenever they were together. No matter how many times this daughter tried to orient her mother to reality by reminding her she was her daughter and not her mother, the mother would blankly stare at her continuing to call her "Mom." "I just can't stand it," she wept. "I am her daughter, not her mother. I can't begin to tell you how much this hurts me . . . and makes me angry. My father died a few months ago and I feel as if I have lost my mother too, when she persists in thinking *I* am her mother. She's *my* mother and as confused and crazy as she is, and even though I have to tend to her needs, she is still my mother and I can't relate to her or think of her in any other way."

The sometimes endless repetition of past experiences and events by old people is considered by many to be further evidence that role reversal does, indeed, take place. This behavior, which we call reminiscence, may at times be quite annoying, but it is never childlike. The expectation that these repetitions should be actively discouraged in our parents because they are unhealthy or regressive in nature is false. According to Robert Butler, chairman of the Department of Gerontology at Mount Sinai Hospital and Medical School in New York City, reminiscence is part of a larger looking-back process called "life review." Butler defines life review as a "naturally occurring, universal mental process characterized by the progressive return to consciousness of past experiences and particularly the resurgence of unresolved conflicts."[11] By recovering memories, both hurtful and gratifying, the elderly individual comes to terms with who she is and the experiences and events that shaped her identity. Life review is a healing process whose impetus is approaching death. Says Butler, "Probably at no other time in life is there as potent a force toward self-awareness operating as in old age." In the course of life review, the elderly parent may reveal to her child or spouse "unknown qualities of her character and unstated actions of her past. Hidden themes of great vintage may emerge, changing the quality of a life-long relationship."[12]

Reminiscence should be encouraged. As a component of the process of life review, it is curative for our parents and may create new levels of intimacy between the generations. If you can no longer bear to listen to your mother's or father's stories, ask someone else to listen. Others who haven't heard their tales are usually delighted to hear them. My husband, brother, and I have listened to my father's stories about what it was like to live in Russia during the Revolution thousands of times. We find ourselves, of late, bored and angry when Dad is about to begin "the saga." Our friends, on the other hand, whom we invite to dinner when Dad is present, find his stories compelling. They listen with complete attention and delight. They are mesmerized by his anecdotes. When the evening ends, they always tell me what a remarkable dad I have. And my father will tell me how wonderful it was for him to "get out and talk." Reminiscence is healthy! By talking about past struggles and hardships as well as triumphs and achievements, our parents are able to bring meaning to the limited, often painful lives they are currently living. Reminiscence is the process by which our parents make sense out of this mystery we call life; it enables them to find meaning and purpose in the years they have lived. And if you will look carefully at yourselves as I have begun to do, you will see that we middle-aged children are beginning to reminisce.

I cannot overstate that what our parents want most from us is emotional involvement. They want to feel and to know that when they need us we will be there. They want also, as noted previously, to feel they are a vital part of the family network—to share the sad as well as joyous occasions that are the core of family life. Aging parents, by and large, notwithstanding those who cannot relinquish control, are happy to opt for a new kind of parenthood. A parent-child relationship based on what a parent can give of herself, which will enrich that child's existence, is what is desired by most parents. Lessons in life learned from years of experience, stories about what it was like "back then," and personal values and beliefs that have given courage and hope through adversity are some of what aging parents want to impart to succeeding generations. A wellspring of wisdom and philosophy awaits children who are willing to listen. What matters to our parents is that one day, long after they are gone, we, their children, will remember and incorporate into our lives what they have taught us. This most personal communication offers not only a promise of immortality to our parents but also, for the here and now, reassurance that the years they have lived hold meaning and purpose.

6

What about Brothers and Sisters?

I N families where there are brothers and sisters, a parent's aging can and will reactivate old competitions and resentments. I must emphasize that this stirring up of "unfinished business" is not abnormal and routinely happens. Caring for our elderly parents is a most difficult, stressful job, and if there are several siblings they should ideally pitch in. If one sibling is extremely distressed over what she considers unfair disparity in the division of caregiving responsibilities between her brothers and sisters and herself, she can and should do something about it. Sometimes just a direct plea for help is sufficient to cause the other brother or sister to do his or her fair share. Other times, a clear communication of angry feelings may be necessary to bring home to the uninvolved sibling that you cannot continue to care for Mom or Dad without her help. One thing is certain: if the over-stressed sibling says nothing, the situation will not change and will perhaps even deteriorate. Sometimes deeply entrenched patterns of interaction between brothers and sisters cannot be changed. After all, how we relate to our siblings and the role each has in the family is determined early in the history of a particular family. Sometimes family conferences led by a professional social worker or psychologist can produce positive changes in families that appear to be beyond help. These conferences will be further described in this chapter.

Let's begin by describing a particular family consisting of a seventy-five-year-old mother and her two children: a daughter who lives nearby and is principal caregiver and a son who lives about three hours away by plane and who over the past ten years has been home maybe ten or eleven times. This son, who had never been too involved in family matters, suddenly decides to visit Mother; he appears on the scene. Now why is he coming home, you ask? First of all, it is not uncommon for a child, who through the years has seemed uninterested in his parent's welfare, to suddenly return home. There are many reasons for this homecoming, of which I will present a few of the obvious. Perhaps this son felt he was never the favored child and hoped his return would bring him this honor. Perhaps it is a last ditch attempt on his part to win approval from a parent who has always withheld it. Perhaps it is a pang of guilt over never having been an involved, caring son. Perhaps an inheritance is the impetus for his return home. Whatever the reason for this son's homecoming, one can be certain it will affect the previously existing balance between his mother and sister.

For the sake of argument let's say that this brother returns home for two reasons: First, he wants to show his sister that he is more reliable, more capable, and can generally do a better job of taking care of their mother than she can; second, there is a little money, and since he hasn't been around much in the past five years, he's worried he might not get enough of it. Mother is still mentally competent and she will see that he really does care if he comes home for a little visit. The desire to show his sister that he can be the better caregiver did not pop up suddenly. Rivalry between them dates back to early childhood, when each competed for praise from their parents. If one received a prize for scholastic achievement in mathematics, the other had to receive an award in a comparable subject. Because this brother and sister saw each other infrequently through the years, their competition lay dormant. Now Mother is frail and ill; Sister has been the primary caregiver, and there is a familiar stirring in Brother, which on some level he does not understand, telling him to come home to show his sister what an incompetent person she is. What makes matters worse for this sister is that while she has been breaking her back and taking time away from her own family and interests to give the best care she can to Mother, she gets little recognition from Mother for her sacrifice. All along, Mother has been praising her faraway brother for his letters, phone calls, cards and flowers on holidays, birthdays, and so on. Never mind that she is doing the marketing, taking her mother to the doctor, doing the laundry, and finding and coordinating homemaker services. In her mother's eyes, her son is the hero, the prince on the white horse.

So, this brother comes home, takes his mother to the doctor or perhaps to another who is "better," tells his sister she is not supervising Mother's medications properly and that generally she really isn't giving Mother enough of her time. In essence, he tells her she's doing a lousy job. Fortunately, in this situation, the brother eventually flies home and things revert back to where they were. The sister grits her teeth and carries on. But alas, this time she may be just angry enough to let her mother know that she would like some acknowledgment from her of the good care she has been providing. This last visit from Brother has finally given her courage to ask for what she deserves.

If, on the other hand, these two siblings live near each other, an all-out battle might occur; a battle waged with ferocity until and even after the parent dies. Each sibling will attempt to outdo, out-maneuver, and sabotage the other, if not with Machiavellian cunning then with outright childish tricks. I have seen one sister remove another sister's birthday card from their father's bulletin board in his nursing home room. I have been the recipient of a phone call in which a sister told me I should prevent her brother from visiting their mother because he stirs her up and makes her sick (never mind that this stirring up was the only stimulation Mother received and loved it).

Or take the disquieting story told by a daughter about her older sister. This particular daughter had always been the favorite of her mother's three children. As her two older siblings, a brother and the previously mentioned sister, reached adulthood, they moved quite a distance away from their mother's home. She, however, married someone from the same town and remained there to raise her own family. As Mother got up in years, this daughter, because of geographical proximity and her favored position in the sibling hierarchy, became Mother's principal caregiver. With the onset of the usual spate of illnesses that affect the elderly, Mother grew frail and infirm. As home care became more grueling and taxing, the daughter was forced to quit her job in order to preserve her own physical and emotional well-being. During this time, all calls for sibling assistance were either ignored or dismissed as hysteria. Finally the older sister did say "yes" to a request for a weekend respite and came to stay with Mother. When the younger sister returned home she not only found a computer printout listing all the things she was not doing or doing wrong for Mother, but in her absence, the older sister had also hired a homemaker, for whom the younger sister was expected to pay. One might argue in this instance that her older sister was doing the best she could, considering that Mother never liked her that much anyway. That may very well be (see chapter 9, "Children without the Gift of Caring"). The point illustrated by this anecdote, however, is that sibling rivalry lasts a lifetime and like dry timber can be ignited into a raging fire when a parent grows old.

Battle lines between siblings are frequently drawn when nursing home placement of a parent becomes a reality. I am reminded of an adult daughter, a dedicated and loving caregiver to her Mother for fifteen years, who was the protagonist in such a drama. Out of courtesy to an older brother and younger sister, for whom even a yearly visit to Mother was too much, this daughter called to inform them that the time had come to place Mother in a nursing home. Furious that she had the audacity to make such a decision without consulting them, they told her she didn't know "what the hell" she was doing and they were arriving on the first possible plane to check things out for themselves.

Lots of not so nice things can happen between brothers and sisters as their parents age. If patterns of interaction are not too entrenched and adult children are mature enough to rise above past resentments, they can ask for a family conference. Family conferences, mentioned earlier, are usually led by a professional in the mental health field. It takes one sibling to insist upon such a gathering. Although that sibling may initially be anxious over asking her brothers and sisters to attend, she will usually be surprised by their positive response. Most will not only agree to come but also will be relieved to air thoughts and feelings in a neutral, safe atmosphere. Of course, some siblings may choose not to attend; that is their right, and they should not be coerced. Family conferences can and do bring pleasant surprises and deep rewards. Very often these conferences are "close encounters," where brothers and sisters genuinely communicate with one another for the first time. Secrets never before revealed and feelings never before shared are laid upon the table and explored. Through these meetings, it is possible for brothers and sisters to achieve a closeness and warmth previously unknown.

Sometimes a family conference can produce a standstill, a cease-fire that may not be an optimal result, but is the best a family can do. I refer specifically to a brother and sister who since childhood were at each other's throats and outwardly competitive with each other. Growing up they received little in the way of nurturance and love from parents who were totally committed to their professional careers. Individually, each sibling was a decent human being, but they could agree on nothing, especially when the care of their frail, elderly parents became the topic of conversation. Any discussion about their parents' needs ended in vitriolic debate. To my surprise, however, they asked for a family conference, which they attended with their spouses. In conference, they were rational enough to admit their bickering had to stop. They, therefore, agreed that each would do what he felt appropriate for their parents but keep distant from each other. They scheduled different visiting days to their parents' apartment so they wouldn't have to see each other. They agreed, however, that when key decisions regarding their parents' future had to be made, they would meet with me in family conference to explore options. This armistice was the best this family could achieve and certainly more beneficial to their parents' well-being than the constant conflict that had transpired before. In fact, this sister and brother are to be commended for being able to shelve their anger and act like adults on behalf of their parents.

A member of my support group who cannot have a telephone conversation with her brother or sister without becoming angry and tearful, finds that she achieves positive results by writing to them. She is a public relations consultant, gifted with words. The following is excerpted, with her permission, from a letter to her sister concerning how to divide living time for Mother fairly between her sister's and her home.

Dear Edna,

The reason I'm writing is that it appears that you and I have not been able to comfortably arrive at suitable living arrangements for Mother. I know you must feel, as I do, that while it is unfair that we must be faced with the joint responsibility for her care, still it is one that neither one of us would want to shirk. Up until now, we have both tried to do what we thought was best for Mother, but it is obvious that we must work together to accommodate all of us.

I've given some very serious thought to our last conversation and despite the fact that we were so upset, there were valid concerns being expressed by both of us. For example, I quite agree with you that the Buffalo winter might be too difficult for Mother. It is true that the weather here is milder and the winters not as long. I think what I was hearing you say was that you would have no problem with her coming during the spring, summer, and fall, (from May through October) and that Mother would remain here through the winter, from November through April. She feels that she would be most comfortable with such an arrangement and seems quite happy that we are making an attempt to work things out this way.

I know that you will be as glad as I am that she has shown amazing progress in her recovery which began while she was staying with you. She is now able to care for herself, including dressing, showering, going up and down stairs at will, preparing her own breakfast and lunch, and sometimes dinner if I leave her the wherewithal to warm up, and generally moving about on her own. She does not as yet lay out her own medicine and sometimes forgets to take the late night pills. Her shaking is pretty much under control, although she still has some weak and shaking days. We are able to leave her by herself for longer and longer periods of the day and evening.

I can only say that I wish she were totally able to take care of herself, which she does not seem able to do. I wish that we could count on Tom for moral and financial support, and I wish that the problem of Mother's care did not exist. We both have full lives and we certainly have great feelings of resentment of having to change our life style. Nonetheless, you and I must reach some level of agreement in dealing with Mom's future.

Please let me know your thoughts.

Where sibling roles are clearly defined in the family and children have accepted these roles throughout the years, the above-mentioned difficulties may not arise. (I say "may" because anything can happen during this time of family crisis.) For example, a sister or brother who has been the family "mainstay" and governed with sensitivity and fairness from this position, will usually be able to continue his or her leadership role. The other siblings, having assumed auxiliary roles in an atmosphere where they have felt included and valued, will not, as their parents age, jockey for position. Brothers and sisters in such a family are able to handle the crisis of their parents aging with the same spirit of cooperation with which they have handled every other family problem.

Conversely, when the mainstay or sibling leader has been authoritarian, leaving little room for input or discussion, there also may be no conflict. The other siblings, having learned that their protests are useless, will resign themselves to a situation that though not preferred, is not worth the hassle to change. It is not unusual in such a situation to hear one sibling say of the other, "Sis has always been boss and that's the way I want to keep it. I've never challenged her and I'm not about to now when our parents are old and frail. When she says, 'Donald, I want you to take Mom to the hairdresser next week,' I say 'sure.' She assigns the tasks and my younger sister and I follow her orders. I can't say I like the situation, I can't say it doesn't make me angry but this is how it's got to be, because this is how it always was."

Sometimes the selection process is simple, based upon the current realities of the family situation. When one daughter in my support group was asked by another daughter why she was chosen over her brother and sister to be principal caregiver to her mother, her reply was this: "Well, my brother lives seven hundred miles away, my sister is divorced and caring for a handicapped son, so that leaves me." Or the choice may rest on which sibling has the most bedrooms in her home or who has the most money. Often, however, the one with the most money is the least willing to be involved, financially or emotionally.

Other times, the selection process is founded on the perceptions adult children have of their parents. Not all brothers and sisters like and love their parents to the same degree; some, in fact, do not like their parents at all (see chapter 9). In one family consisting of four siblings, one brother and one sister, who saw their father as ungiving and selfish, refused to take an active part in caring for him. Fortunately in this particular family, the two siblings who perceived and related favorably to their father understood why the other two did not. As a result, a caregiving plan was designed, in which the two who felt negatively were not expected to give as much of their time and energy. If the opposite had been the case, in that the two siblings who saw their father favorably could not and would not brook the attitude of the other two, then bitter arguments and recriminations would ensue, for which there would be no resolution.

Gender is also a major factor in determining who cares for Mother. In our culture, caregiving is perceived as woman's work. Consequently, sons depend on their wives or sisters to take care of their parents. This attitude was humorously described by a member of my support group.

"My brother has told me very matter-of-factly that I, as a woman, am more naturally suited to take care of our mother than he is. That since I do it so expertly, I should expect little from him for as long as Mother is alive. What bothered me most was that he stated his opinion as if it were a universal law of nature, something akin to Darwin's theory of evolution!"

Attrition in itself can be the crucial factor in determining which sibling should assume the caregiving role. In one family consisting of five siblings, all tried to care for a demanding, self-centered mother, whereas only the middle child succeeded. This particular mother wore out and nearly destroyed the others. Or the destiny of in whose hands Mother's care should lie may ultimately be decided by the sheer futility of a sibling's attempts to achieve cooperation. The words to describe such a denouement came from a firstborn daughter, who said:

> I've tried everything to get my brother and sister to help me with our mother. I've wept, screamed, pleaded, talked rationally and calmly, even flattered and manipulated. They absolutely refuse. They won't take Mom for a couple of weeks to give me a break; they won't give me money, of which my brother has lots. All I get are "nos, I'm too busy, you do it so well, why make a change, Mother is happy with you, you've managed nicely without my financial assistance until now." Well, after all is said and done, I've finally come to the conclusion that when it comes to Mother's care, I must consider myself an only child. It's just something else I have to accept and add to my life.

Another knotty and fairly common problem between brothers and sisters may occur when a parent clearly chooses one sibling over all the others to care for her. That sibling carries the burden of care and although other siblings are available and willing to help, the parent wishes for this specific child to be her caregiver. In telephone call two in chapter 1, where mother blocked her daughter from going to work, this was the situation. Daughter, whom we will call Martha, had three sisters, all living nearby and willing to assume responsibility. Mother, however, only wanted to live with Martha and went so far as to not even allow the other sisters to sit with her when Martha and her husband went out.

Martha was the youngest child in this family, eight years younger than the sister before her, and had been with Mother through widowhood and illness. Over the years, anger and rancor through lack of communication between the sisters built up, giving rise to some very false perceptions about what was really taking place in this family. The other three sisters accused Martha of deliberately excluding them from the caregiving situation so that she could dip into Mother's assets and eventually inherit Mother's money. Martha became angry at them for their mistrust of her, resulting in much bitter feuding. Martha finally could take it no longer. With three children under the age of ten and a job she had to keep to support her family, she needed her three sisters' help to survive. Through a family physician who was treating her for tension headaches, she was referred to me. After seeing Martha a few times alone, I began to explore with her the possibility of calling a family conference. Although Martha initially resisted for fear her sisters would not come, she eventually realized that the risk was worth taking. She nervously telephoned each sister and was surprised to hear that each sister was not only willing but eager to attend, after all these years, to vent grievances. Notwithstanding some of the deep problems that existed in this family, we were able to develop a more realistic care plan in which all the sisters participated, over their mother's protest.

This family is atypical in that usually the chosen child upon whom the parents depend is a firstborn daughter. From an early age, she is selected by her parents to help with household chores and to take charge of her younger brothers and sisters. Often this type of daughter will refer to herself as a substitute or surrogate mother. As she grows older, her parents seek her advice more and more on family and financial matters. They demand of her what they do not demand of her brothers and sisters. They run to her with every problem. She begins to feel she is indispensable to their welfare. At no time, however, will these responsibilities weigh as heavy as when her parents reach old age. Although she has been able to cope before, now she may find herself overwhelmed and stressed beyond endurance by her parents' demands. Such a daughter poured out her feelings of anger and frustration at one of our support group meetings.

> For years I have been the one to do it all. I had to drag my sister with me wherever I went. I had to take her to the movies with me every Saturday, I had to cook supper while she watched TV, I couldn't go to college far away, she could. I took care of my parents' finances from the time I was sixteen. At my wedding, at age twenty-four, I was ready to go out the door on my honeymoon, when my father came running after me to tell me I forgot to sign a check for him. I'm really tired of it all now. You'd think I was an only child, the way my mother calls me for every little thing. My sister always had it good, she was never asked to do anything, everything was always me. Now my sister who lives two hours away has no idea of what I do for our mother. She doesn't understand why I'm always exhausted and complaining. It's as if we have two different mothers, because when my mother talks to her on the telephone she tells her she's feeling just wonderful. Well, last week I called my sister and told her that if she doesn't come down and relieve me, I'm going to commit myself. I told her that I'm really going crazy. I guess I was pretty angry, because my sister said "Sure I'll come down. Why didn't you ask me earlier? I really thought things were okay. I didn't take your complaints that seriously."

Happily, the older sister's clear and direct expression of anger generated some genuine communication between the two women. As it turned out, the younger sister had always believed that her older sister was happy in her role. She revealed that at times she was jealous of what she perceived to be her older sister's favored position with her parents. The older sister, astounded by this knowledge and encouraged by her sister's openness, talked about her long held, deep resentment of the younger sister's easier life since Mom and Dad gave her whatever she wanted. As a result of this open expression of feelings, each sister developed a new understanding of the other. They became closer than they had ever been before. When the sad time came for their mother to be placed in a nursing home, they were able to give each other the much needed emotional support such an occasion demands. As the older sister says, "We are now truly friends. How strange it seems that it took my mother's old age to bring this about."

With these two sisters, a family conference was not necessary to bring conflict resolution. Change was effected by one sister's emphatic assertion of strong feelings never before expressed. Such a stance made the other sister stand up and take notice; made her think about things she had not been aware of. The older sister's surprise at her younger sister's benign response only confirms that one can never mind-read another person no matter how close the relationship. The older sister's risk paid off and is a valuable lesson to all, not just to those involved in the family intricacies of elder care. Don't be afraid to state your feelings! You have no idea how the other party will react. Things will either improve, remain the same, or get worse. If you have a hunch it might be the latter, ask yourself what that might be. In the case of the two sisters, the worst thing that could have happened would have been that the younger sister would get so angry she would completely divest herself from the caregiving situation. Should that have happened, the consequences would not have been so dramatic since the older sister was already providing most of the care. As it turned out, things improved beyond the older sister's most hopeful expectations.

What must be made clear in this discussion of sibling relations is that the situations described here are not abnormal or sick. Old competitions do flare up. Sometimes one sibling is preferred by a parent over another to be principal caregiver. More often than not the sibling who is doing all the work gets the least credit, while the sibling who is doing the least receives the most. These things happen in the best of families and seem to come with the territory as our parents age.

Although sometimes family patterns are too deep to change, frequently the potential for resolution of conflict between siblings does exist. Family conferences are not the only means to achieve sibling unity. Just sharing in an elder parent's care may, in the most natural manner, forge a new relationship between estranged siblings. For example, a brother and sister with a long history of coolness may find themselves drawn together as they talk on the telephone to divide shopping and transportation chores and plan grocery lists. After a while they notice the practical nature of their conversations has switched to more intimate subject matter. Anecdotes shared about their parents and past mutual experiences stretch once terse, businesslike dialogues into prolonged and meaningful encounters. In time, to their delight and wonderment, they are behaving like a family again.

So, good things also happen among siblings as they stand at this developmental threshold where they will soon form the vanguard once held by their parents. As we know, crises become opportunities for growth and change. The aging of our mothers and fathers can present the opportunity to fulfill our parents' most cherished wish: that their children remain close and loving after they are gone.

Do not hesitate to call a family service agency, a community mental health center, a social worker, or a psychologist if you find yourself stuck in situations similar to the ones described in this chapter.

7

The Manipulative Parent

E VEN in the closest and healthiest families, we may come across a manipulative parent—the parent who knows how to push those buttons that catapult the adult child into instant action. Those parents who have been manipulative all their lives, carefully maneuvering to get attention or to get others to do their bidding, are pretty much entrenched in a life-style where change is difficult, if not impossible. Volumes of psychiatric literature abound on these resistant-to-change personalities and they will not be the focus of this chapter. The understanding and management of manipulation within the context of caregiving will be our concern.

Feelings of loneliness and abandonment go hand in hand with old age. Even the nicest mom or dad, when engulfed with such painful emotions, may become manipulative. When parents manipulate infrequently and adult children are aware that a manipulative exchange is taking place, sometimes they are able to handle the situation with humor. An adult daughter, whose widowed eighty-year-old father recently moved into a senior center, told me that Dad called her almost every day now to say, in the sweetest voice possible, that he's not eating a morsel of food in his new living arrangement, and that there's nothing like her home cooking. She says, laughingly, that she knows Dad's trying to wrangle a dinner invitation out of her.

Inasmuch as it is important for him to eat in his new home as much as possible in order to adjust and to meet people, she is fairly firm about not giving in to his manipulations. She says that she listens and deeply empathizes but ultimately tells him that with her busy schedule, Sunday dinner is about all she can manage for now.

After he settles in, she tells me, "I will have him over more often, but I won't let him know that yet. I know that if I give him an inch, he will take a mile. Although he was pretty dependent on my mom most of his life, he's together enough to get my message. He knows I mean what I say; I think he also knows I will never let him down." This daughter knows her dad well. Consequently she is able to set limits from a position of maturity and strength. As I have again and again stressed, parents, more often than not, respond positively to their children's requests and needs if they are presented without anger.

For example, the working daughter who cannot stop her widowed mother from usurping her leisure weekend hours, because of Mother's sharply honed powers of persuasion, is beset with a problem not so benign as the one described above. Mother's manipulation, couched in the right language and tone of voice, touches those nerves in Daughter that generate guilt and "I should" thoughts. The mother in chapter 1 who told her daughter, "If you go away on vacation, I'll die," knew exactly what to say to an only daughter, who all her life felt responsible for her mother's total welfare. Manipulations of this sort, in fact, do not spring full blown; they have a history that predates the parent's aging. They originated in early childhood, with each party responding to cues like laboratory mice conditioned to react to certain stimuli. With the passage of time these responses became almost fossilized in their resistance to change; each participant plays a part with a degree of comfort and indifference. These patterns become second nature; a way of living and being for parent and child until that time when Mother's or Father's aging becomes a reality requiring attention. When the needs of the aging parent become prominent in the lives of the caregiving adult children, troublesome rumblings occur. The promises and hopes of middle age, whether they include going away on vacation or spending time in whatever way you wish, are threatened by the intrusiveness of urgent parental demands. For the adult child who has always placed her needs secondary to her parents' and whose self-worth rests upon being a good daughter (or son), parental manipulation is irresistible.

If you recall, the daughter in chapter 1, the target of those powerful words, "If you go away on vacation, I'll die," was ultimately able to cope with her mother's manipulations by setting limits. Lest you think this was easy for her, remember several counseling sessions were necessary to reinforce and support her right to have time for herself. Such a long-standing pattern will not change merely by wishing it to. Although wishing it to is the first step, the adult child caught in this behavioral interaction may require professional help or the support of a group to produce significant change. Patterns developed over a lifetime do not yield to change overnight. But negative patterns of interaction can be changed when motivation is present, and a change in one party often generates similar positive changes in the other.

The elderly, when fearful of abandonment and loss of control, may use physical symptoms to have their needs met. An elderly mother and her son and daughter-in-law with whom she lived come to mind. This eighty-year-old widow, who otherwise seemed content in her living arrangement with her children, became manipulative whenever her children were ready to go on vacation. She would have heart palpitations and dizziness of such a severe nature that her children initially were forced to cancel several vacations. Because the son was retired and enjoyed taking trips with his wife in their new motor camper several times during the year, these frequent separations became a serious problem. As a clear-cut pattern of vacation-illness, vacation-illness unfolded, the children realized that Mother was feigning sickness to keep them from leaving. They tried confronting Mother with what they thought was going on—that she was pretending to be ill to keep them with her—but she would not hear of this. She became angry and so did they. As they found themselves becoming more and more exasperated, they sought help.

This mother did not have a prior history of manipulative behavior. She was, in better days, the matriarch of her family, strong and independent, the dominant figure upon whom children and grandchildren depended for support and advice. After her husband died, she managed alone in her home until, out of necessity, she had to move in with her son and daughter-in-law. This move was traumatic, as it symbolized a loss of control over her life. Not only was she no longer mistress of her household, but also she felt that the role in which she took the most pride, that of parent, was stripped from her. She was now living in her children's home and, on a level she could neither understand nor express, felt her world was topsy-turvy. To gain some semblance of mastery over her painful situation, she resorted to manipulation. If she could still be a parent powerful enough to direct her children and to get attention from them, all would not be lost; life would still have some purpose.

When her children understood the source of her manipulation, they were able to help her and themselves. Rather than confront her with her hypochondria, as they had previously, they acknowledged the severity of her physical symptoms by taking her to their family physician as soon as she complained. The physician, sensitive to the needs of the elderly and knowledgeable about what was happening, gave her a thorough medical examination and reassured her that all was okay. Furthermore, he gave her his telephone number and insisted that whenever she felt palpitations when her children were away, she was to call him immediately. She also had my telephone number and the reassurance that I would visit her at least once during her children's absence. An involved grandson who lived nearby and a medic-alert medallion worn around her neck gave her an added measure of security. With all this attention to and fuss over her own needs, she was able, though reluctantly, to accept her children's needs for rest and recreation. A solution was available from which all parties benefited.

When the sources—usually fears of abandonment, loneliness, and loss of control—of parental manipulations are understood, the adult child is in a stronger position to deal with the behavior. Moreover, manipulations, if allowed to continue over a period of time, will only produce anger and hostility, and as I have already noted, will transform the art of giving care into a joyless chore, devoid of gratification and love. Manipulations, if not maturely handled, will eventually create distance between parent and child. The following illustration comes to mind.

An adult daughter, whose job in a neighborhood shop allowed her to have a leisurely lunch in her own home several times a week, would find her seventy-eight-year-old widowed mother, who did not live with her, waiting for her in her kitchen when she arrived. She was in a rage at her mother, not only over this intrusion, but also for the abuse of the privilege of having given her a key to her house. She was silent about how she really felt because her mother never ceased praising her for her devotion and love. Mother's words were: "What would I do without a daughter who understands me so well? Without you my life would not be worth living." She was so afraid of hurting her mother's feelings and so guilty over her anger that she decided her only option was to give up the pleasure of dining at home and return to eating lunch at work. "It is the only way I could get away from her without hurting her," she said. Her rage, however, continued. As her resentment grew over the sacrifice she felt forced to make, she was aware that whatever closeness she once enjoyed with her mother was gone. Sadly, too, she noticed that whatever affection she was able to demonstrate to her was at times ungenuine and tinged with anger. Had she been able to confront Mother honestly about her needs, Mother's feelings may, indeed, have been hurt, but in all likelihood Mother would have come around to accepting her daughter's position.

I reiterate: elderly parents, above all, want to be loved by their children and, as a rule, will bend if they are approached by them with confidence. And had this mother not relented, her daughter, at least, would have had the satisfaction of knowing she had the self-worth not only to express her needs but also to refuse to participate in a manipulation that would benefit no one. Such a posture is considerably healthier than being engulfed in the kind of interminable anger that only guilt can spawn.

An example of how to successfully confront a manipulative parent is provided by Judy. Judy, age forty-eight, is the primary caregiver to her eighty-year-old widowed mother. Judy's mother lives independently in her own apartment, where she manages nicely with a few hours of daily household help. She is in reasonably good health—able to bathe, tend to personal hygiene, and prepare meals. Although she does not drive a car, friends in her building take her wherever she needs to go. Judy has a husband, a sixteen-year-old daughter who lives at home, and is a full-time bookkeeper.

Judy's mother is difficult in that she likes lots of attention and feels Judy should be doing more for her. That most of her concrete needs are met by friends does not satisfy her. She would rather that Judy meet her needs. Because the role of parent is a major component of her identity, Judy's mother derives a sense of control and power from knowing that she can still give Judy orders that Judy will follow.

Judy's mother has a way of conveniently forgetting that Judy has a full-time job, and an insidious pattern has developed whereby she will call Judy on a weekday night to ask a favor for the next day. She will open with, "Darling, I have to go to the bank tomorrow and I wondered what you were doing then. I'm counting on you taking me, since there's no one here to do it." Or she will call Judy on a day off, when Judy has planned something for herself and say, "I know you're off today and I thought how nice it would be if we had lunch and went shopping. I hardly ever see you." Judy usually rearranges her day to please her mother. She feels unworthy and guilty if she turns her mother down. She has tried to tell Mother how pressured she is, but Mother never seems to hear.

Judy came to me and then to our support group wiped out and in tears. She felt manipulated and powerless. With the support of others who had solved similar problems, and after several group sessions, she risked saying the following to her mother:

> Mom, you have got to stop calling me to do things for you without advance notice. I would be delighted to take you to the bank or out to lunch but you must let me know earlier, so that I can tell my boss. Please recognize once and for all that I have a job, where my time is not my own. I also really resent that you take my availability for granted. You never ask if I have time. It's always, "Will you please do this or that." I have a busy life with lots of responsibilities which you prefer to forget. You also forget that I see you every week and call every day. Unless you learn to respect my needs, I will not see you as often as I do.

Judy's mother heard her this time! Valuing and needing her daughter's love and respect, the phone calls stopped. Over a *planned* lunch a week later, her mother resignedly said, "You've changed. You're no longer a little girl." The ultimate outcome was a closer relationship in which Mother eventually revealed to Judy her feelings of uselessness, and Judy was able to demonstrate in words and actions how much she still needed her mother's friendship and support.

It is well to remember that it takes two to make a successful manipulation: the manipulating parent and the manipulated child. If the adult child does not bite the hook, the parent is stunted in her effort to get the child to do what she wishes. The adult child may initially feel guilt in not acceding to his parent's dire pleas, but in time this emotion will lessen as the adult child notices that Mother or Dad no longer resorts to childish artifices to have her or his needs met. As adult children feel more confident in "being adult," and their parents sense this, a trusting climate is established in which communication of needs takes place without fear and defensiveness, and genuine understanding develops. In such an atmosphere, manipulations are no longer necessary.

8

Seeing Our Parents
as People

S OMEPLACE along the pathway to maturity, there should come a
time when we cease seeing our parents as idealized figures to be
feared and worshiped, but rather as people no different from us. To
be able to see the real human being behind the parental facade is part
of the separation process that produces fully grown-up adults. If we
have not achieved this developmental milestone early in the life
cycle, the aging of our parents presents us with a final opportunity.
The attainment of this goal—to see the person behind the parent—
is not easy.

Throughout our lifetimes, most of us continue to perceive our
parents as strong, infallible figures, who are usually right and with
whom we must always agree. As our parents and we age, it is imperative that we begin to look at our parents as vulnerable human
beings with imperfections and needs like anyone else. If we can learn
this new way to view our parents, we will be able to cope more
maturely with their behavior. Not only will the process of caring for
our parents be eased by this new perception, but with the absence
of fear, intergenerational communication will also be vastly improved. After all, how can we gain understanding of our parents'
needs if, paralyzed by their magical powers, we are too intimidated
to ask necessary questions? How can we enjoy a relationship with
our parents based on mutual respect if, like adolescents, we continue
to see them as authority figures to be rebelled against and proved
wrong? And how can we set limits if we retain childish fantasies of
parental punishment and rejection every time we say no to them?

We cannot really help our parents during their crucial years of need and dependency if we perceive them as tyrannical figures to fear and please at all costs. We cannot be dependable caregivers unless we are first and foremost fully mature, separated adults.

The process of separation leading to adulthood begins in infancy. It is a gradual movement away from the mother, upon whom we are totally dependent. With increasing emotional and physical capabilities, we learn to walk, to feed and dress ourselves, to entertain ourselves; generally, to spend more and more time away from the original source of our need fulfillment. Eventually, of course, separation becomes more pronounced as we go away to school or to work or to marry and have families of our own. In this process of separation, if all goes well, the magical powers over life and death we once thought our parents had, disappear. We begin to see our parents as people, like us in some ways because we spring from them, but also unlike us, because in our movement away from them we have become separate, unique individuals—we have become ourselves.

What happens during the old age of our parents that affords us, their middle-aged children, another opportunity at separation and maturity? As our parents experience physical and mental decline, they turn to their children for support. The role reversal described in chapter 5 officially begins, challenging us to be dependable caregivers. Just as with siblings, old patterns of interaction and unresolved conflicts, usually emanating from the separation process, resurface to interfere with the caregiving process.

If children have not been able to separate by the time their parents reach old age, those who feel responsible for their parents' total happiness and those who cannot say no, for fear of parental reprisal, will burn themselves out as caregivers and feel resentment and guilt. Those who persist in seeing their parents as authority figures to oppose on every issue will be able to neither assess their parents' needs with objectivity nor deal compassionately with their dependencies.

Children who are stuck in some earlier developmental stage will continue to see their parents as parents and, as a result, will not have the insight to cope maturely with some of their outrageous behavior. On the other hand, children who are able to see their parents as people know there are some things about their parents that will never change and will instead use their energies in situations where potential for growth exists. Some adult children who have learned to understand the source of their parents' strange doings are, likewise, able to turn seemingly impossible situations into mutually satisfying ones.

Understanding how important it is to his father to be an authority on matters pertaining to restaurants and food, an adult son I know, who is a true connoisseur, told me that he has finally given up arguing with his seventy-three-year-old dad over where to dine whenever they eat out.

I am secure enough now to allow Dad his selection. I would always get so angry that he would never let me choose which restaurant to eat in, we'd have bitter battles; occasionally I would win, but it wouldn't pay because he'd complain about this or that throughout the entire meal. Well, I no longer need to be right. You know, in his heyday, he was one of the largest wholesale meat distributors in this area. I appreciate and understand how good it makes him feel to consider himself an expert in his field, so to speak. Now that all that rebellion stuff is over, I really have a good time with him, even though it means eating some pretty bad food. I feel I have achieved a victory.

He has, indeed, achieved a victory, a magnanimous one, born of his ability to see his father not as a tyrant to overthrow, but as a human being with a deep need to be valued for his particular knowledge. In what may appear to some as a game of charades, this adult son allowed his father to be an expert knowing that his acquiescence would bring to his dad a degree of pleasure he otherwise could not give him. His acknowledgment of this expertise, so crucial to his dad's identity, was a gift whose full meaning can only be savored within the barren confines of old age, where so little exists to bring gratification.

Always keep in mind that the elderly are stripped of so many roles so quickly—spouse, provider, friend, employer, property owner, and so on—that what seems trivial to us may be of great consequence to them. As previously mentioned, the most meaningful gifts are affectional, affirming to our parents that they still count as human beings; that they still have something of value to offer. It is worth reemphasizing that this son's willingness to change resulted from his ability to let go of childish things. He no longer had to prove his father wrong. Furthermore, he was able to see him as a person, for whom acknowledgment of his role as "expert on dining" was important. A gesture of this nature is certainly "taking care of Dad" in its most noble sense.

There is another piece to seeing our parents as people. This facet has to do with making a deliberate effort to develop an understanding of our parents as they were before our births. After all, they were people before they became our parents! Knowledge of the events and experiences that shaped their personal histories can only help us to recognize what in their personality structures is receptive to change and what is not. Such knowledge, furthermore, frees some adult children of feeling responsible for certain parental behaviors. Additionally, children who are able to see their parents as people do not squander energy on relationship issues that are resistant to growth. Instead, they center their efforts on "positives" that promote closeness and affection. Of course, the understanding and appreciation of our parents as people can only be accomplished if communication is open and we are unafraid to ask the necessary questions as a prelude to mutual dialogue.

The importance of seeing parents as people became personally beneficial while I was taking care of my mother during her last few years of life. As firstborn daughter to immigrant parents, I early on assumed the role of protector and mentor in their new culture. I was completely tied up with their welfare, genuinely believing that I had the power to make or break them. To illustrate, if I did well in school, they would be happy; if I did not, I would cause them irreparable unhappiness. If I had the "right" friends, I could protect them from the hurt of social rejection because they had funny accents. These irrational beliefs were reinforced by my mother's personality which, as far back as I can remember, was characterized by a somberness of mood. She always looked sad, as if her heart were the seat of the sufferings of all humanity. That she was blessed with intelligence, humor, a love of music and art, and an infinite capacity to understand others all got lost for me in her aura of melancholy. I truly felt I was responsible for her sadness and that I had it within my power to heal her. Because we were close and as a result of psychotherapy, I eventually learned to understand the source of her pain—years of material hardship with complete loss of childhood and its irreplaceable joys—and to take pride in her enormous human strengths. She really did not need me "to make it"; in fact she had already made it without me and was still making it. What a relief! I was free at last to relate to my mother as friend, not protector.

During the last five years of my mother's life, however, she developed Parkinson's disease. The muscle rigidity caused by this cruel disease gave her face a cast, the likes of which made her earlier countenance seem cheerful by comparison. Now she *always* appeared angry, and I found myself unconsciously reverting to old thoughts and patterns. Was she angry because I wasn't visiting her enough? Was she angry because I was planning a vacation? Was she angry because she thought I should be doing more to make her happy? Fortunately, before turning these thoughts into impulsive actions, I had the good sense to ask her what she was feeling. Of course she was angry, she said; not at me, but over the dreadful fate that was in store for her. She affirmed for me what a wonderful, caring daughter I had been, and for the first time told me that all her life she felt people missed knowing her true nature, because they judged her by the ever-present serious expression on her face. Imagine what my caregiving relationship with my mother would have been like if I had not gotten to know her as a person; if I had not taken the time to develop a feeling for the soil that bred her.

A visit to the South Boston neighborhood where her Irish mother spent the first twenty-five years of her life helped a caregiver daughter in one of my support groups to understand the essence of her mother's personality.

I know where my mother's fury comes from. Seeing that street where her house and the houses of her aunts, uncles, and cousins still stand, I know why she didn't want to leave after she married my father. She was surrounded by love and security all the time. There was always someone to be with, to talk to, to eat with, to run to when things were rough in her own home. I wouldn't have wanted to go to New Jersey either, to live in my husband's strange land with his strange family. Look at all that warmth and protection she left behind. No wonder she's bitter and always talking about how things have never been the same for her since she left Boston. She just can't let go of her old life. I can see why my father and she eventually had to separate. That trip gave me real insight into her personality. I used to think I was the cause of her fire. Now that she is old and I am the one to care for her, it is important that I understand her as a person. I know what cannot be changed.

Seeing a parent as a person became critical for Harry when his seventy-five-year-old otherwise healthy father experienced bowel symptoms that required in-hospital, invasive tests to rule out a malignancy. Harry's father flatly refused these procedures on the grounds that it was his right to do so. He told Harry he had no right to interfere in this matter or to coerce him to do the opposite of his wishes. Harry, an only child, had a close relationship with his father. He was, however, sufficiently separated to understand and relate to his father as a person rather than as a figure to be feared or never questioned. Because he knew his father's personality, Harry was able to convince him to get the care he needed. He knew his father's resistance was not a "rights" issue but was determined by a long history of anxiety about anything to do with doctors and hospitals. With lots of reassurance from Harry that he would be at his father's side whenever possible and from the physician that the procedures were not risky, Harry's father had the tests and the resulting bowel resection. Had Harry been afraid to stand up to his father, his father would not be alive today, enjoying an active, full life.

Even when separation has occurred and we relate to our parents as people, it is often difficult, especially as we witness their aging, to surrender the notion that they can no longer be the strong, vital people they once were. We are never completely prepared for the emotions that snap at us at the most unexpected times. An adult daughter, very "together" and grown-up, related to me how on an occasion when her eighty-year-old mother and she were walking up the stairs to their favorite ice cream parlor, her mother very stridently reminded her that she was, after all, old, and could use a helping hand to navigate the steps. Exclaimed the daughter, "I couldn't believe I was racing in front of her like that. I guess there's a part of me that wants to deny she's getting old, that she needs my help."

This denial assumes serious proportions when it actually interferes with appropriate treatment for a parent. An adult son, fifty years of age, close to his seventy-six-year-old mother all his life, could not accept nursing home placement for her. She was becoming mentally confused to the point of wandering around her apartment building at night, knocking on strange doors, stocking up on food but forgetting to eat, and not changing her clothes. A daughter, who lived nearby, had a more realistic hold on the situation and urged her brother to consider nursing home placement. Alzheimer's, in fact, was suspected by the mother's physician. The son questioned the doctor's diagnosis, insisting that if Mother had more to keep her busy she would be fine. Moreover, he expressed that his sister was railroading their mother into a nursing home because she never liked Mother anyway, and this was the way to get revenge.

Mother had been an accomplished cellist and music teacher most of her life. At a very early age the son learned to play the violin, and their mutual passionate interest in music created a strong bond between them. Until Mother's decline, whenever the son would visit, which was at least twice per month, in spite of the two hundred miles that separated them, they would play duets. He loved his mother very much. She was a source of great pride and inspiration to him. He often told me she was the most remarkable person he had ever known. He could not bring himself to see her as a seriously ill woman who needed more skilled care. He tenaciously fought nursing home placement, even spending weekends to take care of her, neglecting his own family. Her decline, however, was very rapid; with the onset of incontinence, the die was cast. He was inconsolable in his grief, eventually requiring professional help to bring insight to his unique relationship with his mother.

Caregiving cannot be governed by irrational forces from the ancient past. Rather, it must be defined by the variables of our needs and limitations and those of our parents. We cannot sort out and assess these variables if childish disturbances clutter the pathways to realistic solutions. Perhaps the secret to mutually satisfying caregiving lies in this chapter. Learning to see our parents as people with personalities separate and distinct from ours enables us to use the information and follow the guidelines outlined in this book. Setting limits, establishing realistic goals and expectations, putting brakes on frenzied caregiving, "being with our parents emotionally," permitting our parents to take necessary risks, preventing manipulation, understanding our anger, and ultimately, becoming the kind of dependable caregiver inherent in the true meaning of role reversal, all become possible with the mastery of this task.

9

Children without the Gift of Caring

ELAINE BRODY,[13] in a moving piece of writing, talks about adult children who are unable to give care to their parents because they, themselves, did not receive the "gift of caring" from them. The degree to which all of us can care and love depends to a large extent on what we were given by our parents somewhere along the line. Those children, blessed with parents who rode out every disaster at their sides, have been instructed in the art of caring. Those children with parents who actively delighted in and were interested in their triumphs and achievements know what caring is all about. Those children who have never experienced similar nurturing in most cases cannot give it back to their parents. As Brody points out, to judge those children bereft of this gift as bad, unloving, or uncaring is harshly unfair. Not all parents have been or can be loving, nurturant, and supportive of their children. For such parents, in their old age, to expect their children to furnish them with the affectional supplies they never gave them in the first place is unrealistic and unjust.

I vividly remember a case conference at a nursing home where I was the social work consultant, at which the physician in charge voiced his disappointment and anger toward the adult children of one of the residents, because they rarely came to see their mother. One of the nurses, knowledgeable about the history of the family, immediately spoke up in defense of the children. It seemed this parent, who had always been totally self-absorbed and ungiving, deprived her children of all warmth and affection throughout their life-times. The nurse went on with example after example of the mother's and father's withholding of affection, complete preoccupa-tion with their own needs, and physical and emotional abuse. She concluded her diatribe by saying, "They should be applauded for coming whenever they did. Were I they, I wouldn't have visited at all!" Children without the gift of caring, whom I have personally counseled, amaze and impress me in what they do for their elderly parents. Like the nurse at the case conference, I believe they deserve praise, not shame.

An adult daughter, whom I'll call Helen, came for help because, although she was a dependable caregiver to her father, who had Alz-heimer's, to the point of dividing his living arrangement with a granddaughter (yes, the next generation is involved too), she could not stop herself from feeling an intense anger, at times bordering on hatred, toward him. The images of her father coming home drunk, squandering his paycheck on his own pleasures, and not being with her mother during a particularly serious surgical procedure blazed in her consciousness, standing in the way of her giving care with a willing and charitable spirit. She was not able to forgive him for his unreliability as a father and husband. Her guilt over harboring such dark feelings was exacerbated by constant comparison with friends and others who were able to care for their parents without the bit-terness she felt was tearing her apart. She began to experience a pervasive feeling that not only was there something seriously wrong with her but also that she was at the very core of her being a "bad" person. She would ask me over and over again, "Is there something wrong with me, Vivian, because I can't care for my father the way I feel I should?"

With individual counseling from me, combined with the group support of other caregivers, she was able to free herself of this ter-rible guilt. Recognizing that because of the circumstances under which she had been raised, she could not feel otherwise toward her father—indeed, it was natural to feel as she did—she began to feel good about herself again; that she was a decent, kind human being.

Several years ago when I was a clinical social worker in a geriatric assessment unit,* an attractive, meticulously groomed eighty-two-year-old mother and her equally attractive fifty-three-year-old daughter came to our office for a comprehensive evaluation of the mother's medical, emotional, and social functioning. The daughter brought in her mother because Mother was neither sleeping nor eating and was complaining of vague abdominal pains. She had already taken Mother to several physicians who were unable to shed light on her symptoms. Because we were specialists in geriatrics, she came to us for answers.

I still remember this mother and daughter, not only because each was so strikingly physically attractive, but because initially I was fooled by their outward behavior into thinking they had a close, loving relationship. The daughter gently held her mother's arm as they

---

*Geriatric evaluation units can be found in most major cities throughout the country. As a rule, they operate out of hospitals, where staff and testing facilities are readily available. The core of the GEU is a team of three professionals: a physician, nurse clinician, and clinical social worker. With these three entirely different disciplines at work, the geriatric patient (and her family) is assured of a comprehensive assessment of her functioning. As knowledge about old people expands, specialists in the field have come to recognize the importance of understanding the geriatric patient holistically, not merely in terms of her medical problems. This kind of in-depth assessment can only be achieved by a team approach, which is central to the concept of a GEU.

Our team consisted of the three above-mentioned disciplines. Our procedure was that I would see the patient first to obtain a thorough psycho-social history. Upon completion of this piece, I would confer with the other two team members about my findings. Their medical evaluation would follow my initial interview, after which we would meet again to put our collective data together. The result we hoped to achieve was a treatment plan, based on the realities of the patient's life, which would enable her to function with appropriate independence and compassionate support in whatever her living arrangement was at that time.

The psycho-social part of the evaluation, my piece, consists of two parts. The first is the gathering of information about how the older person is "making it" in her environment. Is she getting out and connecting with others; does she have visitors, how often and how many; does she make and receive phone calls, how often and from whom; does she have family, how involved are they in her life, where do they live? Additional knowledge about what the environment offers her in terms of community supports (transportation services, homemakers, meals-on-wheels program, and so on) and whether she utilizes these resources is also obtained in this part. The second part, psychological in nature, refers to how the geriatric patient feels about herself. Does she like herself; does she feel useful, loved, and wanted; does she have interests and activities that lend pleasure to her day? Or does she feel lonely, depressed, and afraid that others are out to do her harm; does she feel no one really understands her? What kind of coper has she been; how has she managed through life's inevitable disappointments and losses? Of course, both parts are inextricably linked, in that if someone is lonely and depressed and sees the world as ungiving and hostile, she will neither be able to reach out to friends and family nor avail herself of community supports.

entered my office and they chose to sit next to each other on the sofa rather than on two separate armchairs. However, as the mother began to respond to my questions about her personal psycho-social history, the daughter visibly stiffened. Although she made only a few pertinent remarks while her mother spoke, always politely deferring to her, the coolness between the two became evident to the point where it was almost palpable. The mother, intelligent and verbal, was able to tell me in a clear and forthright manner exactly what she felt and thought. She was angry, she said, and felt abandoned and alone.

> My daughter, who is sitting beside me, brought me here from my home in New England to take care of me. I lived in _____ most of my married life, had many friends there and my older daughter lived not too far away. Well, my husband died ten years ago and five years later my daughter. When she died they should have buried me with her. My son-in-law remarried, and he and his second wife moved away with my grandchildren to Chicago. Though all these things were terrible, I was able to manage. I had my church and some volunteer activities to keep me busy. I don't know why she brought me here. I'm depressed and my physical condition is worsening. I have to use a cane now, as you can see. I have to contend with homemakers I do not like and my daughter is always going on trips with her husband.

She continued with a host of other complaints, all related to her daughter's selfishness and her own current ungratifying life situation. Upon completion of my part of the assessment, including consultation with the other two team members, the mother was ready to undergo the second part of the evaluation, a full medical work-up. While the mother was being examined by the physician and nurse clinician, the daughter returned to my room asking if she could speak with me. She did not want me to think she was a terrible daughter after all the things her mother had said; she wanted to set the record straight.

The facts as she presented them were quite different from her mother's account. She told me that her mother had always been a loner and a most difficult person. "She was a cold woman who never allowed anyone ever to call her by her first name." After her first daughter, who was her favorite because she looked like her side of the family, died, she was indeed devastated, wanting to die with her.

> All my life my mother always let me know there was no way I could measure up to my sister. When she died, although she never said it, I had the distinct feeling she wished it had been me. On the basis of my mother's treatment of me throughout the years, I could not feel otherwise. If you are wondering where my father was through all this, he was there, that's about all. My mother ruled and he passively went along with her wishes. I brought my mother here, because she could no longer remain where she was. She had no one there who really cared. At least here she would have my husband and me and my children, who, when they are home, visit her. We share holidays together and I do the best I can, considering she gave me so little. She would like me to see her every day; I will not. She resents that my husband and I share many interests and do lots of things together. Every time we go away she falls into a state of semi-collapse. I will not be manipulated by her. My husband comes first, and that's how it's going to stay. I feel very little guilt, because in my heart, I know that considering all things, she's lucky I do as much for her as I do.

There were tears in my eyes when she finished her story. She is an example to adult children with parents who have not been able to present them with the gift of caring, that positive adaptations are possible within an intrinsically negative caregiving context. Fully appreciating the complexity and depth of her coming to terms with such painful emotions, I asked if she was able to do all this soul searching without professional help. She told me she did see a social worker for a little over a year, but that her husband's unwaivering support is what really made the difference.

The medical part of this mother's geriatric assessment, incidentally, revealed nothing significant. She had mild arthritis, good hearing and vision, and diabetes that was under control. Mentally she was alert and completely oriented. The abdominal pains turned out to be of unknown origin, which ruled out the possibility of malignancy. Her problems were due to depression resulting from anger over feeling abandoned by her daughter and that life had cheated her.

This mother was not only an uncaring parent but a "difficult" one (see chapter 14). No amount of pandering to her needs by her daughter, homemaker, or any significant person in her life could alter her personality or satisfy her. Considering the minimum of love and real care she gave to her daughter, her daughter's attitude that "she's lucky I do as much for her as I do" is realistic and mature.

That all children should care for their parents remains a powerful dictum. Even those who consider themselves sensitive and compassionate can be rigid in their beliefs of what others should do. Consider, for example, what happened in one of my support groups when Sandy became a member. Everyone knew from the outset that Sandy was different—she did not feel close to her mother and even seemed to dislike her. Although Sandy described episodes from her painful childhood to the group, they did not hear her. Rather than support her or give her recognition for what she was doing for Mother, they urged her to do more and to try strategies that worked with their parents. Since Sandy's relationship with her mother and her family history differed markedly from theirs, the more involved care the group insisted that Sandy should render was not feasible. The care they forced upon Sandy could only flow from a reservoir of love, which Sandy and her mother did not share. Eventually, the group learned a few things from Sandy: that relationships between parent and child differ; that what works for one caregiver may not work for another; that like most caregivers, Sandy's best was good enough.

The emotional involvement talked about in chapter 2 is almost impossible for children without the gift of caring. To expect such children to reminisce with their elderly parents and share thoughts and feelings with them in an atmosphere of warmth and love is unfair. The reservoir of positive emotions necessary for intimate engagement does not exist. To require that these children pretend what they do not sincerely feel is stressful and produces additional guilt and anger. Whatever emotional support the adult child feels she can genuinely give is good enough, including not giving any at all!

The concrete or instrumental caregiving chores are easier to manage, as they do not entail high levels of intimacy and are usually time limited. Taking a parent shopping, doing the laundry, or balancing the checkbook do not require emotional investments. One does what one can to help Mom or Dad with a specific chore and then leaves. The adult child has the clear sense that he is making a difference in his parent's limited life, without experiencing the stress of forced emotional involvement. Concrete support choices afford the adult child without the gift of caring the opportunity to be the dependable caregiver embodied in the true definition of role reversal (see chapter 5).

Because an adult child is unable to be loving in her role as caregiver does not mean that she cannot be loving in other roles. Nor does it mean that she is "bad" or ungiving at heart. Adult children I know who are not able to care for their parents as they had ideally wished achieve success as parents, grandparents, and friends. They are devoted and sensitive parties in these key relationships. In the role of parent, especially, as a result of their personal struggles, they are determined to do better by their own children. What they dread above all else is a replica of the relationship they had with their parents.

10

Who Comes First?

"WHO comes first? My aging parents or my spouse?" This question is central to some of the more painful conflicts inherent in caregiving to our parents. Since it is adult daughters who provide the bulk of services to their frail, elderly parents, the context of this chapter will be mainly in terms of the strains and choices wives experience and perceive as they try to meet the needs of the two generations that flank their middle position. Although it may appear to the reader that I am pitting Husband against Mother in this chapter, such unhealthy competition is not my intent. My emphasis is the *couple relationship* and the importance of preserving it under what at times is unbearable and unremitting tension.

In answer to the question, "Who comes first?" my reply is: your husband! The obvious reason for this stance is that time is running out. Since most adult daughters who render care to their parents are between the ages of forty-five and sixty, and some even older, it stands to reason that the number of "vertical" years (as opposed to "horizontal" or lying-in-bed years) is dwindling. Middle agers want to live as fully as they can while they are healthy and vigorous. Myrna Weissman,[14] in her Yale University studies of women and depression, has shown that women do not become despondent during the "empty nest" stage of the life cycle, but rather exult over the long-awaited reprieve from child care. For men, as well, middle age promises increased leisure time and marks the end of the "empty pockets" phenomenon. With no more college or other education bills to pay and with children who are finally on their own, there is cash left to indulge in a few luxuries. Though some marriages in middle age end in divorce or separation, most husbands and wives view these years as an opportunity to recommit to each other. With the pressure of raising children over, many couples are able to enjoy new levels of intimacy, both emotional and sexual.

One husband summed up the essence of middle-aged marriage thusly: "It's just wonderful. It's more than being able to sleep with the bedroom door open again; it's the freedom of space and time which is now ours. If we feel like going out to dinner we can, because we don't have to cook for kids anymore. If we want to go away for the day, we can return home whenever we want. Above all, we can talk or be silent together without children to intrude. Middle age is a last chance from God or whomever, while we still have health and stamina, to live life fully." (For adult children who have neither married nor had children, middle age basically holds the same meaning. It is a time for pleasure, relaxation, and dream-fulfillment.)

For spouses in a second marriage, middle age adds yet another dimension. As a remarried couple who raised seven children in the same house for fourteen years, my husband and I hailed the day our last child left home as a landmark event. Our friends in first marriages arrived at that blissful juncture way ahead of us, and we were ecstatic at finally catching up. For the first time we had our house to ourselves—without kids. Sadly, though, my mother's diagnosis of Parkinson's disease coincided with the departure of our seventh child. My running back and forth (sixty miles, round trip) twice each week to care for her and relieve my dad cut into our long-awaited couple time. Although I loved my mother deeply, I became resentful. Would it never end for us? Would we ever be able to act like "a real middle-aged couple?" If caregiving responsibilities continued to increase at this rate, we ourselves would be in wheelchairs before we were granted respite.

These precious years, however, pass swiftly and the autumnal needs of married couples for enjoyment are urgent. Consequently, husbands can and do become resentful of the time their wives spend in elder care. The marital tension precipitated by these intergenerational conflicts takes on added poignancy at this time of life. As a result, when mates voice their anger and irritation, it is time to talk, to set things straight, to assess the damage and plan repairs. There are always ways to negotiate, to compromise, to bring balance and harmony back to the couple bond. At this stage of the game, a state of war is hardly what married couples need or wish. Couple unity is more important than ever, and it need not be sacrificed in order for daughters or daughters-in-law to be dependable caregivers to their parents.

A second reason for advocating "spouse first" has to do with separation and growing up. As I mentioned in chapter 8, life is such that we must to a degree separate from our "families of origin" in order to begin our own lives as fully adult persons. With separation, we are able to proceed to the next stage, where these earlier attachments become secondary to those of our generation and the next. We emotionally invest in these new attachments, particularly in the next generation, because they in a sense represent our immortality. If we do not have children and grandchildren, then we give of ourselves to our interests, causes, and other human concerns. In other words, as the natural order of life, the needs of our own families eventually are given priority over those of our parents. If we are not able to effect this kind of separation when we ourselves reach old age, we may look back with bitterness and regret upon our middle years as unfulfilled opportunities. Of more importance, without this growth, memories of our parents will be tarnished and sour, as we blame *them*, rather than ourselves, for these wasted years.

Not surprisingly, most elderly parents, if asked "Who comes first?" would respond with, "your husband, of course!" As noted in chapter 2, elderly parents want their children to prosper. They rejoice when their offspring are blessed with good marriages and healthy and happy children. More than anything, they want their children to live fulfilled lives, and they do not receive pleasure when their children make sacrifices at their expense. The last thing most parents want to witness is marital or family discord that they feel they have caused by their intrusions and demands. Many a parent, sensitive to such conflicts, has said something like this to me: "Oh, I would never make such a request of my son. His wife wouldn't like that at all, and I don't want to start any trouble. God forbid."

The irony, however, is that whenever an elderly parent may be the cause of marital or family disharmony, he or she usually does not know it. And by the time he learns of it, the situation has flared to crisis proportions. Although Husband may complain that Wife is devoting too much time to Mother, or Daughter may be angry because Mother broke a shopping date to take Grandmother to the doctor, Grandmother herself is ignorant of these sore spots. No one

has said a word to Grandmother about what is happening; if someone had, chances are she would have set things straight right away.
Adult children must tell parents how they are feeling before matters
get out of hand, when it becomes impossible to communicate in civil
tones. Based upon the proposition that elderly parents do not want
to be a burden or cause distress to their children's families, in all
likelihood they will understand and do everything in their power to
improve the existing situation.

In my work with families, the few husbands (mostly wives and
daughters come for help) I meet lend emotional and some concrete
(rides to and from doctors' appointments, marketing, help with
household chores, and so on) support to their wives' caregiving efforts. Given the opportunity, they will listen to their wives' grievances, acknowledge the stressfulness of their situations, and frequently be skillful problem solvers of intergenerational conflicts.
One reason I've noticed why these husbands can be supportive is
that they simply are not emotionally deprived as a result of the addition of caregiving to the long list of their wives' chores. Women,
conditioned to be nurturers, adept at meeting the needs of many and
at promoting and sustaining harmony in key relationships, are able
to give their husbands sufficient attention and affection to satisfy
them. These women artfully hide from their spouses their anguish
and conflict. At great expense to themselves, in terms of physical
and emotional well-being, these wives run their households as if
nothing has really changed. The issue of "Who comes first?" never
comes to the surface, because these wives are burning themselves
out in an effort to put *both* generations first. They are doing it all!

An attractive and highly capable fifty-five-year-old daughter in
my support group, whom I will call Ruth, has been caring for her
seventy-nine-year-old mother in her own home for almost seven
years. Mother has suffered a stroke and, although ambulatory and
able to take personal care of herself, she cannot assist with most
household chores. Ruth, who has a full-time job as a buyer in a
department store and cooks meals and does laundry every day, is
married to a demanding husband who expects her to be there for
him at his beck and call. Their marriage is consequently a traditional
one, in which the husband will help when asked, but essentially
there is a rigid division of labor—matters of the hearth belong to the
woman. When Ruth returns home from work she doesn't sit down

for a minute; when she tries to snatch a few minutes of privacy, either her husband or mother is with her. She says, "Some days they follow me from room to room and the only way I can be alone is to visit a neighbor or go to the movies." Yet, neither Mother nor Husband knows how distressed Ruth is. On the surface, she appears to be tending to everyone's needs with ease. Ruth says she has hidden her feelings well over the years because she does not want her husband to resent her mother's presence in their home. "My mother and I have always had the closest relationship. When she had her stroke, I knew right away I wanted her to come live with me and she wanted the same. I want her with me till the end. If my husband knows how hard it is for me he might want her out."

She is, however, now beginning to detect flickers of anger that cause her pain and guilt. She is intelligent enough to understand that she must talk about these negative feelings or else she might become sick. Consequently, she elected to come to support group meetings, where she can at least vent her emotions, although she is certain she can never change her existing situation. She is truly Elaine Brody's "Woman in the Middle," caught in a cross fire between the demands of her husband, mother, job, and even her children and grandchildren. Like many other women, she explores the possibility of quitting her job (12 percent of working daughters in America quit their jobs to take care of their elderly mothers) to cut down on chores, but inasmuch as her work gives her both fulfillment and respite from family pressures, she has wisely chosen not to do this.

This "doing-it-all superwoman" behavior, as we know, is unhealthy, and if allowed to go unchecked can make a caregiver ill. Such women are better advised to take the risk of telling their husbands their fears. They may be pleasantly surprised by a supportive response from husbands whose capacity to care and empathize was grossly underestimated. If, on the other hand, the husband's response is angry and nonempathic, in all likelihood the situation will not worsen from "putting the cards on the table." First of all, the wife will feel instant relief from the expression of long-suppressed strong feelings. The daily subterfuge, eroding her physical and emotional well-being, will finally be at an end. Second, an up-front open confrontation may even result in the couple obtaining professional counseling. Often a neutral third party in the form of a clinical social worker or psychologist can bring new perspectives to a seemingly hopeless situation. Certainly, if Mother were apprised of these goings-on, she would not tolerate them. Again, the last thing our parents want is to be the cause of marital discord among their children. In the above case example, if the relationship between Mother and Ruth is as close as Ruth describes, then it will surely withstand honest, straight talk without either party falling apart. This daughter, however, in spite of support group efforts to convince her to open up intergenerational communication, remained resistant to change.

Another daughter who was "doing it all" and not getting away with it because her husband would not stand for the intrusions in his life, found herself forced to change or else forfeit her marriage. Joyce, sixty-two, the only child of an eighty-six-year-old mother, came to me conflicted and in tears because her husband was totally unsupportive of her wish to keep Mother in their home. Joyce described her mother to me as sweet and undemanding, and she could not understand why her husband did not view her the same way. According to Joyce, her mother was "the easiest person to have around the house." Joyce's mother had lived in Florida for the past twenty years, where she had friends and a full life. Summers, however, were spent with Joyce and her husband, Martin. In September, she would return to Florida, usually accompanied by Joyce, who would stay with her for a few days to help her settle in. Although Mother had suffered several mini strokes in the past three years, she was still able to manage well on her own. Last summer when she came to stay with her daughter, she appeared more frail, and on an occasion when Joyce and Martin had to be away for a long weekend, Mother broke her hip at the respite-care center where they temporarily placed her. Mother made a remarkable recovery and within three months was able to use a walker and attend a medical day-care center three times a week. Joyce did not mind helping Mother dress or get ready for bed, nor was she unwilling to prepare meals, since she had to cook for her husband anyway. Heavy-duty personal care, such as showering and bathing, was done at medical day-care. Although Joyce admitted to experiencing stress and some anger caused by having to be extra patient with Mother's slowness, she felt that she was generally coping.

As summer turned to fall and fall to winter, it was apparent that Mother would not be able to return to Florida; her days of independent living had come to an end. By then Martin was growing uneasy over Mother's protracted stay. He complained about having to share their one and only bathroom, was put out by his mother-in-law's continued presence at the dinner table, was furious over his loss of privacy, and worried that they would be forced to sacrifice yet another vacation because of his mother-in-law's declining condition. Still smarting from the cancellation of their fall holiday plans, Martin was fearful of a repeat performance. Resentful and angry, Martin told Joyce she would have to place Mother in a nursing home. He informed her there was no way they were going to miss this vacation and she had better make plans for Mother's care outside the house, as he would have no strangers in his home while they were gone. Well, Mother had broken her hip eight months earlier in a respite-care center and Joyce, understandably, was not about to place her in another one.

When I first saw Joyce she was distraught.

> My husband doesn't understand what my mother means to me. He was the youngest of six children and always cared for. I am an only child and since my mother was widowed twenty-two years ago, I am all she has. He's asking me to make a choice between her and him. I don't know what to do. I cannot hurt my mother and I love Martin. We've had a good marriage. Why doesn't he understand my feelings for my mother? Maybe you could talk to him and convince him to be more reasonable. And besides, my mother is so sweet and good-natured; she's really no trouble to have in our home.

Joyce and I spoke for quite a while that day. She was deeply distressed and in her distress felt isolated, without anyone with whom to talk who could understand her pain. I explained that her dilemma was indeed serious, in that her marital happiness was at stake. I felt, however, there was a good chance we could find a solution if Martin and she would come to see me for further exploration of the problem. Her first response was that such a meeting was out of the question as her husband would never come. She later reconsidered, realizing she should at least ask Martin. Martin, who was as distressed as Joyce, was the one to call for an appointment. I saw Martin and Joyce as a couple twice. I saw Joyce individually several times and later in support group meetings. I also met with Mother on a home visit. Happily, before their spring vacation, we arrived at a resolution to this painful problem.

What made resolution so difficult was Joyce's strong attachment to her mother. Some place along that developmental road, when Joyce could have separated from her mother, she did not (see chapter 8). She felt irrationally responsible for her mother's well-being and was so sensitively attuned to her mother's moods that when her mother was depressed, Joyce herself could not enjoy the day. Had Martin not forced the issue of Mother's future, Joyce might have remained stuck in this developmental rut. Her husband's insistence on "doing something" forced her to reexamine priorities. In essence, he was saying, "Her or me; it's time to grow up."

Joyce was so timorous of hurting her mother's feelings that in the eight months Mother had been in their home, she did not initiate discussion on anything pertaining to future living arrangements. In fact, Joyce continued to pay the rent on Mother's Florida apartment. The effect of Joyce's inability to confront Mother on Martin was that he felt he no longer counted in Joyce's eyes—that his mother-in-law came first. Enraged as Martin was, he was smart enough to realize that if Joyce put Mother in a nursing home to please him, the resulting rift would permanently damage their marriage. He knew such a decision had to come from Joyce and her mother for reasons besides his own pique. Martin felt immobilized; he saw no way out. Until Joyce openly talked with her mother, they were at an impasse. Of importance is that the history of Martin's relationship with his mother-in-law had always been positive. He liked and respected her as much as Joyce. When she first came to stay in their home, he was supportive of Joyce's caregiving efforts. Only when the likelihood of her leaving became doubtful did Martin bristle.

A compromise was reached whereby Martin allowed someone to come into their home to stay with Mother the six weeks he and Joyce would be on holiday, in return for Joyce's talking to Mother about realities and options. Vacillating in her resolve, Joyce required lots of support to fulfill her end of the contract. Finally appreciating that she could not have her marriage and her mother, that her commitment to Martin was of first order, she told Mother that caring for her was proving to be too much and was cutting into her personal life. How did Mother react to this pronouncement? She said she felt such a move was in the offing; that although she was content in her daughter's house, she knew it wasn't good. Her words were: "I may not have good ears, but I'm not blind and I saw things between Martin and you I didn't like. I probably should have said something, but I was selfishly hoping all would work out."

Mother did go into a nursing home after Joyce and Martin returned from vacation. Joyce continued coming to support group sessions and saw me occasionally for individual counseling. In time she was able to verbalize how truly burned out she was from caring for Mother. She told the group that her anger had reached the point where she was happiest when Mother was at day care. "I used to stand at the door at least fifteen minutes before the van would pull into the driveway and then feel guilty after Mother left because I was so pleased to be alone." These were hard words for Joyce to utter; to her they implied not only betrayal of her mother but also of her self-image of what constitutes a good daughter. Joyce, however, had the courage and inner strength to face her feelings and work them out. No longer torn by the Martin-Mother conflict, she was able to give her mother the quality care she wanted her to have; care whose source was joy rather than guilt.

A more attractive reason why some husbands are supportive of their wives' efforts to care for their elderly mothers or fathers is simply that they wish to be. They are committed to their wives and respect their concerns. Indeed, if the marriage is a healthy one, where spouses can listen to each other nondefensively and trust each other enough to share vulnerabilities, husbands can frequently be helpful in bringing a more realistic perspective to the caregiving situation. The husbands with whom I have had professional contact very matter-of-factly tell their wives when they feel taking care of Mom or Dad is cutting into valuable couple time.

A fifty-two-year-old daughter who had been visiting her father in his retirement community twice per week and spending lots of time on the telephone with him every day was told by her husband that she was overdoing it and that the intensity of her caregiving was producing visible strains in her and in their marriage. He told her that he was beginning to feel very left out and wondered if they could talk about what was going on. He related the following:

I didn't say, make a choice between Dad or me, that would have been childish. But it seemed that every time we sat down to dinner or were having a nice chat, her father would call with his latest complaints, after which she would be too upset and spent to enjoy our time together. Also, I was beginning to feel like I didn't come first anymore. Well, we've always been open with our feelings and I simply told her mine. So, we took Dad out to dinner one night and told him what was bothering us. And you know what? He said he was sorry and glad we told him. He additionally told my wife that visiting him twice per week was really too much—once each week would make him just as happy.

This husband was able to help his wife see when a caregiving situation was getting out of control and, as a result, was enormously helpful to her in setting limits.

Furthermore, when husbands lend active emotional support to their wives' caregiving chores, wives tell me that it is their spouses' empathy that enables them to make it through the caregiving ordeal. "Without my husband's love and support, I would not be able to do it," is what I've heard over and over again. If husbands can provide some concrete help as well, such as taking Mom to the doctor or shopping, this is better yet. Nevertheless, the proffering of emotional support alone from husbands is enough to make a difference. Indeed, whenever a daughter–caregiver is about to make a major decision regarding a parent's care, in terms of increased personal commitment, I always ask where her husband stands on this matter. If the husband is not able to give a modicum of emotional support, I advise her to consider other options. There is no question that some kind of co-partnership, some kind of sharing of responsibilities, not only reduces pressures on the wife but also minimizes if not curtails marital strain.

Of compelling interest is that when sons are primary caregivers to their elderly parents, they do not experience the same stress as daughters. Recent research by Amy Horowitz of the Brookdale Center on Aging[15] has provided important evidence to show that sons were less likely than daughters to feel that they had to sacrifice leisure time or give up anything because of caregiving responsibilities. Horowitz reported that generally fewer sons than daughters experienced the negative emotional effects of elder care. Additionally, according to Horowitz, "Men were significantly more likely to name *their wives* (italics is mine) as one of the other relatives involved in providing care to their parents than were the adult daughters to report that their husbands were involved." In other words, the emotional and concrete support given by daughters-in-law to husbands who care for an elderly parent was a crucial variable explaining why sons generally perceived caregiving as less stressful than daughters.

The implications of Horowitz's findings for this chapter and this book are noteworthy. First, they illustrate the importance of co-partnership in caregiving. If wives could depend on their husbands for concrete and emotional support in caring for their parents to the same degree husbands depend upon wives, "Who comes first?" need not be asked, and wives would not be at great risk of "burn-out." Second, it raises the entire issue of daughter-in-law stress. How does it differ qualitatively and quantitatively from daughter stress? Certainly care given from marital obligation rather than biological bonding would produce added strain on the caregiver. Daughters-in-law cannot be expected to feel the same closeness toward their husbands' mothers as toward their own. Blood is indeed thicker than water, and "Ruths and Naomis" are rare. The repository of love, affection, and loyalty produced by a lifetime of shared family experiences allows a daughter to say what's on her mind or to resign herself with humor to a difficult parent's incessant demands. Either way she can temper her resentment. However, a daughter-in-law without a long history of familial gives and takes with her husband's mother may have to bite her lip under similar circumstances.

One daughter-in-law whose mother-in-law lives with her told me: "If she were my mother I would have told her long ago to behave herself. As it is, I go into my bedroom to punch pillows instead of her. When my husband's home, she is, of course, delightful, so my husband doesn't believe me when I tell him what she does in his absence." The marital strain produced by such dynamics must be dealt with head on and, if necessary, explored in counseling sessions.

The problem is that marital tension created by daughter-in-law caregiving rarely reaches the counselor's ears. If it is difficult for a wife to tell her husband how conflicted and torn she is in caring for her own mother, imagine how much more so it is for a daughter-in-law who cares for her husband's mother. She would opt to live with the strain rather than bring the emotions to the surface for exploration and help. Remember too, as I mentioned in chapter 3, because women are socialized to be nurturers and please others, they will continue to do it all rather than call attention to their plight. "Who comes first, your mother or me?" are easier words for husbands than wives. Furthermore, as Horowitz posits, since the daughter-in-law is shouldering most of the caregiving burden, it is doubtful that her husband feels the same pull on the couple bond that she does. If he is not feeling conflicted or stressed and she has chosen to remain silent about her needs, why see a counselor?

The point is that the couple relationship does come first. Healthy, fun years are dwindling for middle-aged caregivers, and it is part of the process of human growth and change to tend to the needs of their generation and the next. Moreover, our parents, who have lived a long time and have the wisdom to appreciate the value of close relationships, would be the first to tell us to live as fully as we can with our spouses during these middle years. It is what they want for us too! So, if it is your parents' permission you need to put first things first, you have it. In fact, you even have their blessings. Above all, remember that to be a dependable caregiver—to be there for your parents when they need you and to be there for them emotionally—does not mean you have to place your marriage on a sacrificial altar.

Do not hesitate to get help from a clinical social worker, psychologist, pastoral counselor, or any qualified professional in the mental health field, if these issues have become prominent in your life.

11

That Unexplained Anger

W HAT about that surge of anger we feel toward our parents at the most inexplicable times: an anger that we cannot understand, feel has no rationale, and would like to admit does not exist? We may label it as irritation or frustration, but make no mistake, it's anger. This book is not a discourse on how difficult it is for most of us to express anger or how guilty and pained we feel if we do give vent to this most feared emotion. There is much helpful literature available on this subject. I will only deal with it here as it relates to adult children and their parents. I want to say outright that it is normal to feel some anger at some time as we and our parents together navigate this crucial developmental stage. Even if the relationship between adult child and parent has been close and loving, the adult child will feel anger if she will allow herself to be open to it. It is an anger born of the recognition that our parents can no longer do for us and that we must now do for them. Again, in a sense, as I have mentioned before, it is an anger born out of the realization that our childhood is over.

For me, the painful awareness that I was angry at my mother occurred one noontime when I arrived at my mother's apartment and realized there was no beautiful lunch waiting for me on her table. I would usually come on my day off, sit down with my father to dine, and she would, with what I can only describe as pure joy, serve and watch us eat. Oddly enough, however, long before that day, she had already stopped cooking lovely meals and I had more and more found myself in the kitchen doing the actual preparation. In retrospect, I now remember brushing off whatever uncomfortable feelings I had then as irritation or annoyance. So unwilling was I to admit anger at my mother's inability to perform the most nurturing of all tasks—feeding me—that I irrationally persisted with the idea that soon things would be better. On that day when the final awareness hit me that my mother would never, as she once had, prepare lunch for me, I was able to allow myself to feel rage at losing an important way in which my mother expressed her love for me. I also realized how much I still wanted to remain a child and I was deeply ashamed. I later learned from clients and friends that my anger was not unnatural; that most adult children at one time or another experience it. One adult son told me that he felt it when he saw the stains on his once fastidious father's trousers; another, when her mother was no longer interested in hearing about her children's accomplishments. Both felt shame and guilt over their anger at such petty things.

That we must do for our parents at a time when we would prefer to pursue our own interests is another matter with which we must reckon. Vacations long dreamed about and planned for must be postponed. Anticipated trips to visit distant grandchildren must likewise wait until Dad gets used to his new home-health aide. Even an evening dinner with friends may have to be cut short because tomorrow you are driving one hundred fifty miles to take your mother to the doctor. Sometimes it seems that the subject of *all* your conversations is your aging mother or father. Under such circumstances, it is easy to become angry.

During one of my support group meetings, when we were deep into an exploration of angry feelings toward our elderly parents for not behaving like parents, one of the members, through tears and trembling, made the following statement.

I am crying because I have allowed my father to take such a large chunk out of my life with my husband. Steve is now sixty-seven. A lot of his friends have cancer and heart problems, some have died recently. If he should die soon, I don't know what I'll do with the resentment and anger I have towards my father . . . and at myself for letting him intrude so much into our lives. After Dad's last hospitalization, I was such a fool to let him stay with me for so long, almost two months! He took over our den, which was always Steve's special room, monopolized the TV, and managed to stick his nose into our personal conversations. He even sat in

Steve's chair. I could see Steve get more and more agitated and frustrated over what was going on, though he never said an unkind word about Dad. And for the first time there was a real strain in our marriage—a real distance between us. I love my dad, but my life with my husband is what counts now.

In response to this, another younger member said:

I know what you're feeling. I am forty, married late, had my first child two years ago, and have a fourteen-year-old stepson from my husband's former marriage living with us. I want to enjoy these precious years of watching my baby grow and of doing fun things with my husband, but I can't. Since my mother died, my father has become mentally confused and forgetful. I spend most of my time managing his financial affairs, obtaining homemakers for him, doing the marketing, taking him to the doctor, that I find myself angry as hell at him for not getting his act together and helping me out. I know it's irrational to feel this way, but I do. Why can't he do all these things for himself? Why didn't he take care of his affairs early on so that I wouldn't have this burden? I love him, but I'm really mad at him for needing me so much at a time of my life when wonderful things are finally happening to me.

The anger and resentment are there. Make no mistake about this. Mother can no longer prepare lovely meals or be there in a pinch when we need her for some emergency. Dad cannot even keep his clothes clean. Mother no longer shows an interest in what her grand-children are doing. Our parents simply cannot do and give as they once did. Let's face it, we are angry because our parents are not behaving like parents. It just doesn't seem fair that at this time of our lives, when we've finally been granted some time to live, our parents won't let us. They consume and take up so very much of our time, which is running out.

We are, however, distressed and ashamed to admit we feel such negative emotions. Instead we write off what we feel as annoyance or irritation—anything, but not anger at our parents for letting us down; for growing old. Relabeling or denying what we feel will not help us manage our inner turmoil. We know in this day and age that anger suppressed can make us sick. Suppressed anger causes depression, backaches, headaches, and gastrointestinal disorders.

Loving our parents and being angry at them at the same time is not an entirely new inner experience. Most of us have been able to cope with this mixture of feelings without too much discomfort throughout our lives. When our parents age, though, and the finiteness of time for us and for them becomes a painful reality, the fusion of these opposite feelings may present emotional disturbances requiring help. It then becomes necessary that you have someone with whom you can talk about the anger and the pain you feel over your parents' aging.

I have mentioned support groups many times in this book. Indeed, a good portion of my material is derived from actual stories told by members of my support group for children of aging parents. A major benefit of these groups is that they afford individuals the opportunity to be with others who are experiencing similar dilemmas and emotions. We all feel much better about ourselves when we learn we are not unique in our misery; that others out there have the same unacceptable thoughts and feelings as we do. Irvin Yalom,[16] professor of psychiatry at Stanford University, calls this aspect of support group process "universality." He pointedly refers to it as a "welcome to the human race experience."

Anger toward a parent, especially a frail, elderly one, easily falls into the category of "unacceptable feelings." Those harboring this emotion irrationally believe they are "bad" daughters and sons who have failed to achieve proper filial respect. After all, the mandate to honor thy father and mother does not include a clause saying it's okay to be angry at them for getting old or for making demands upon our lives, or for constantly reminding us that soon we will be where they are. Given the almost taboo-like aura surrounding the expression of anger, is it any wonder that the adult child involved in giving care to an elderly parent would rather bottle it up than give vent to it? How could anyone in his right mind reveal to anyone else that he is absolutely furious with his seventy-eight-year-old mother for calling him every time she has an anxiety attack? How could anyone possibly understand his anger toward her for one minute telling him that she wants him "to be happy, to live his own life" and in the next breath saying, "I haven't seen a soul all week and you are all that I have." Seated at a support group meeting listening to others spew similar rage and reveal similar experiences, the caregiver knows that here he can tell it all. Because others in the group feel as he does, he can risk self-disclosure; he will not be judged or humiliated. At best, he will receive from the group the sublime validation that he is okay; that he is a good and lovable human being.

Longtime support group members who initially came to the group terrified to reveal their own anger at a parent are adept at sniffing out this inhibition in others. They are often more successful than I in encouraging someone to "get it all out." The example of Lois comes to mind. Lois had come to the group three times before she was confronted by Marjorie, an alumna of many group sessions. Lois, who was caring for a manipulative mother who was totally insensitive to her needs, would respond with a smile and a few Pollyanna phrases to questions from other members concerning how she was managing. During one of these customary exchanges, Marjorie interrupted with some of her own opinions on the subject of Lois and her mother.

> My God, I can't believe you're not in a rage over all the garbage your mother pulls. How can you sit there these past few weeks and tell us that you're managing. Your mother reminds me of mine. I used to be like you, afraid to admit that there were times when I wanted to kill her. But I've learned that "anger, stuffed" can make you sick. I also realized that to make up for the terrible guilt I felt over being angry at my mother, I would increase my caregiving responsibilities beyond what I could realistically handle—in the long run, making me even more angry. I know that under your lovely smile, you're smoldering. Listen, it's okay to say you're mad at your mom; we're all in the same boat here. You're a caring daughter and being angry at your mother doesn't cancel out your devotion and all the wonderful things you've done and are doing for her.

Lois reacted to Marjorie's exhortation by denying that she felt any of the things Marjorie described. At the next meeting, however, almost before we had a chance to sit down, Lois told us, with a sense of real relief that Marjorie was correct, that she *was* furious and Marjorie's prodding finally enabled her to confess her feelings.

In this context, it is appropriate to mention that there are two kinds of support groups: those that have leaders and those that do not. Many support groups function successfully without a professional leader or facilitator. One that comes immediately to mind is

Alcoholics Anonymous. Support groups for adult children care-givers, however, work better with a leader. A psychiatric social worker, psychologist, or pastoral counselor knowledgeable in the psychology of aging, developmental psychology, and family systems theory can offer fresh understanding and insight to adult children stuck in seemingly unresolvable conflicts. The clinical wisdom of the experienced professional, moreover, is essential to the establishment of a nonjudgmental group climate in which adult children, already burdened with excessive guilt and "shoulds" and "should nots," can feel safe in revealing their innermost feelings.

Support groups are bound by rules of confidentiality so that members have reassurance that whatever they say will remain within the confines of the group. Many members, nevertheless, choose to become friends outside of the group, offering support to one another in times of crises.

The caregivers of our generation (I am fifty-five) were raised to be "silence is golden" junkies. We were taught at a tender age that angry feelings in general, and toward a parent in particular, are bad and should not be voiced—better to bite our tongues than to speak. Consequently, we have come to regard anger as an emotion to dread rather than accept as one of the many feelings that makes us fully human. Only by accepting and understanding the meaning of our anger will we be able to forgive ourselves and not feel ashamed. The recognition of our vulnerability as human beings will enable us to love and accept our parents for what they are and for the anger and pain they must endure at this stage in their life cycle.

12

The Hardest Decision of All

WHAT is the hardest decision adult daughters and sons have to make in the process of caring for their elderly parents? It is, of course, the decision to place a parent in a nursing home. It is something we do not want to think about, and our wish is that our parents live relatively functional lives until they are ninety, and then just die suddenly without pain. In fact, we wish this for ourselves, do we not? No arthritis to stiffen and permanently immobilize our hands and feet; no Alzheimer's or other form of dementia to disconnect us from our lively world; no cancer to ravage us with unrelenting pain; no stroke damage to render us overnight a nonperson or at best a wheelchair one. Nothing, absolutely nothing which will take us from our homes to alien places where alien people will place their hands upon our bodies. A curse on any of these horrible afflictions— they are not going to happen to us or to our parents. But the sober fact is that they will, and some of us (the percentage is 6 percent of those over sixty-five) will end our lives in long-term care facilities, more commonly known as nursing homes.

The decision by an adult child to place Mother or Father in a nursing home is an infinitely painful one. Psychologists postulate that the emotional aftermath is far more devastating than the grief reaction experienced by the adult child after a parent's death. This finding certainly makes sense, inasmuch as we know from an early age that our parents will not live forever and that one day we will be without them. We can accept this reality with a certain philosophic calm. After all, we will not be the cause of their dying. We are, in a sense, innocent bystanders to a natural process, over

which we have little control. We are not, however, on the sidelines
when we are called upon to place a parent in a nursing home. At this
point we are active participants, struggling with an overriding feeling that we are committing a terrible act; that at best we are acces-
sories to a major crime, something akin to willfully and deliberately
extinguishing our parent's life.

Unlike death, which is final, nursing home visits to our parents
are a constant reminder of the cruel thing we have done. Every visit
brings to full consciousness our sadness and pain. If we are close to
our parent, the pain is unbearable. If we are not, if our feelings
border on ambivalent or hostile, the pain is still palpable and
can be destructive. Even if the family is a close one and the decision to "place" is made with full consent of the parent, the adult
child's emotional turmoil is all-consuming and crippling. After
placement, adult children find themselves depressed, unable to sleep,
prone to crying spells, unable to concentrate, and often anxious
and irritable. Said one adult daughter member of my support
group:

> I am always thinking of my mother and what's happening to her
> there. Are they taking good care of her? I used to feed her myself
> to make sure she would eat enough and walk her daily for exercise.
> I am afraid they're not doing these things as well as I did or at all.
> And I always kept her in clean fresh clothes every day. How can I
> be sure they're doing this in the nursing home? I know that when
> she has to go to the bathroom they are never in time. Once I found
> her soiled. My mother is always on my mind and I am continu-
> ously depressed. I keep thinking there's something I could have
> done to prevent this terrible thing from happening. I feel I am the
> cause of her loss of personhood and dignity. I am always feeling
> either guilty or angry and often both at the same time. I just know
> I could have done something to keep her home.

In the case of the daughter mentioned above, whom I will call
Irene, the fantasy that she could have done something to keep her
mother home was conscious. When questioned by other group members about what that something was, she responded with a litany of
ideas, none of which were practical or realistic. I would like to list
some for you.

1. "I could have quit my job to care completely for my mother until the end of her life."

2. "I could have gotten her around-the-clock help. Even though I can't afford it, I could've taken a loan or a second mortgage on my house."

3. "If I didn't do the above, I certainly could have redoubled my efforts to be with her more—before work in the morning and after work around five. I don't know though whether my husband would have appreciated such a time sacrifice."

4. "I could have had Mother come live with us, in which case I still would've had to quit my job. And it probably would have been the end of my marriage had Mother lived in our home."

As the group explored these thoughts with her week after week, she gradually came to understand that nursing home placement was the only alternative. Of immense personal help was her review with the group of the placement process beginning with the first time her mother fell and Irene was called at work to come to her mother's side. Successive falls, increased frailty and dizziness, loss of appetite, more calls to the workplace and early-morning calls to her home, the unreliability of home-health aides, the onset of incontinence, and Irene's own unremitting stress and anxiety from running in too many directions convinced her that a skilled care facility was the only realistic option. As she put it, "At that painful point, I knew all roads led in one direction only, toward a nursing home, but how was I to speak of this with Mother?"

Because the relationship between Irene and her mother was close and honest, they had been able to talk about the possibility of placement three years before it actually happened. Although these early discussions helped to pave the way, Mother would still become depressed whenever the subject was broached. In her heart, Mother hoped that with aides and companions she could remain in her own home until death. In Irene's heart rested the same wish. In the end it was Mother, in fact, who called Irene one evening to tell her she felt it was time to "say goodbye to my home." Irene was astounded by her mother's admission and described to the group her relief and sadness over the final resolution. The hardest decision of all had been made in a matter of minutes over the telephone—not by Irene but by Mother herself. It was the end of one era and the beginning of another.

The point is that the advent of nursing home placement does not lessen the adult child's stress. The nature of the stress is altered, but the stress itself remains. Although a daughter like Irene no longer has to shop and market for Mother, or take her to the doctor or worry whether the aide will show up or whether Mother has taken her medications, she now finds herself beset with a cluster of new and different problems.

Perhaps the very first dilemma is how can she clean out Mother's house and disburse her personal possessions when Mother is still alive? After all, these things are done only after someone has died! A member of my support group tore at all our hearts when she described the day she and her sister went to Mother's apartment to clean it out. On that day (deliberately postponed as long as possible) when they entered their mother's home, they experienced a grief and sadness that they could only describe as paralyzing in its power. She related that for an indeterminate amount of time she and her sister held on to each other and just cried. When they were sufficiently steeled to sort through Mother's clothing, jewelry, treasured memorabilia of old birthday cards, graduation programs, camp letters, and newspaper clippings, they realized their sense of betrayal and guilt was too great to do the necessary job. They felt they had no right to invade Mother's personal domain while she was still alive. How could they make decisions about what to save and discard without picking up the telephone to call her? There was no question in their minds that if Mother were dead this whole process would be a lot easier. They finally decided to keep what they considered the essential things and hire a person to finish the rest. At the end of their story, another group member, an only child, commented, "At least you had each other. I had to do it alone. And besides the pain, I felt a terrible rage at my mother for not having discarded more of her possessions earlier. Even my father's high school term papers had been stored in a trunk. It was not fair that these painful decisions about what to keep and what to let go were left to me, while my mother was still alive."

Second, how does the adult child cope with the heavy sense of loss and pain that bears down upon her day after day? Would frequent visits to the nursing home lessen her agony and helplessness?

In the beginning, she may take this route, eventually to learn it does not make her feel any better. To the contrary, as she notices the difficulty Mother has settling in, she becomes even more depressed. Each visit produces graphic evidence of the staff's neglect. She hears from Mother of a nurse's caustic tone of voice; she is appalled at the choice of Mother's roommate—a woman who screams day and night; she notices some of Mother's undergarments are missing; she is aware they are not walking Mother enough and leaving her alone in her room for the major portion of the day. There is no question that Mother is declining—she's feeling worse, looking worse, and behaving worse since "placement." She has never seen Mother so full of despair. How could she have taken Mother from her home where she was in total control of her life and placed her in the hands of uncaring, callous strangers? The feelings of guilt, anger, and sadness still grip her; the stress, though different, still eats away at her gut. Frequent visits are certainly not curative for Mother or for her.

Now, in the midst of this emotional turmoil, her husband suggests that, since Mother is finally in a nursing home, they can take that long-awaited and much needed vacation. Is he kidding? How can she? If she went away, her mind would not be at ease. She is perplexed; she doesn't understand; she thought she would feel relieved and less stressed after Mother's move to the nursing home. Not so. Her mother needs her now more than ever. For now Mother is in the hands of others over whom she has no control. She has got to be there to make sure these others do right by her.

Nor does the emotional pounding diminish when an adult child must place a parent suffering from dementia. The adult child still experiences infinite pain, helplessness, and guilt. In fact, these feelings may be heightened because the parent, bereft of the mental ability to make judgments, must turn to the adult child for help. In many instances the demented parent may be widowed, leaving the adult child no one with whom to share this awesome responsibility. The despair continues and intensifies with each visit until the time comes, and it does, when some form of acceptance or letting go occurs. Whether the parent is hopelessly confused or mentally intact, the adult child must resign herself to "this is how it has to be." If she cannot master this task, she must seek help in sorting out her feelings so that she can come to terms with the decision that had to be made and be at peace with herself.

What about sorting out these feelings? How do we do it? And what feelings are we talking about? Is it ever possible to achieve a measure of self-comfort while confronted with the presence of a parent in an institution, about which we have the most negative feelings and into which we feel we have put him?

The sorting out and identification of feelings is not a simple process. Unlike removing a card from a deck and instantly recognizing it as a king of hearts or a ten of clubs, we cannot label feelings quite so facilely. Certainly we know when we are happy, because happy feelings are positive, pleasurable, and easy to stay with, in terms of focusing upon them for understanding. Happy feelings, after all, make us feel good about ourselves. Unhappy feelings, those which, to the contrary, cause us to feel bad about ourselves, are more difficult to allow into consciousness, because they hurt and often cause us to feel anger, shame, or guilt.

When we place a parent in a nursing home, we are buffeted by negative feelings. We feel *guilt*, because we think we could have done more, done something, devised a better plan, anything, to keep our parent in his own home. We feel *shame* and betrayal, because "good" children simply do not abandon a parent to the care of strangers. We feel *anger* because it has come to this: that our parent got old, got sick, that we were forced to be part of this cruel decision and then tend to all the painful details (paperwork, housecleaning, sale of property) such a decision entails. The final upshot, of course, is that we feel guilty over being angry at our parent—the anger-guilt-anger cycle again surfaces in our lives. Our parent's life, once so rich and diverse, is now shrunk to one room, a bulletin board, and a few treasured possessions. The hardest decision of all, in which we played a major part, brought them to this state of dependency and degradation. The pain is steady and breaks our hearts. How do we cope with such debilitating feelings?

These feelings can be managed, however, if we are willing to hold on to them for exploration and understanding. By holding on, I mean focusing on them for as long as it takes to arrive at their clear meaning. Since these feelings are hurtful to us, we do not wish to think or talk about them. Yet thinking and talking are precisely what we must do to achieve mastery over their destructive power. A confidante, be it friend or spouse, may be the one to hear you out, to listen to your pain. If not, a support group, where others are experiencing the same emotions, may provide a safe place to lay your feelings on the table. If relations between parent and child are marked with a history of strain and ambivalence, a sorting out and exploration process is essential, or else the adult child will carry a burden of guilt for as long as she lives. As previously made clear, even when the adult child–elder parent bond is close and loving, guilt and pain may be intense enough to warrant scrutiny and even counseling.

In the case of Irene, a support group was able to help her sort out and understand that those expectations that molded her fantasy were unrealistic, generating feelings of guilt and betrayal that tormented her. With group support, Irene was eventually able to appreciate that as a daughter she did all that was possible to keep Mother at home, and had she put into action some of her fantasized plans, she would have surely destroyed herself. The reinforcement of the group for almost a year helped Irene to let go of her guilt, by which time her mother had settled in in her new home. Without the overload of guilt, Irene was able to plan a more sensible visitation schedule and again enjoy her own leisure time.

Although nursing home placement is less stressful for involved parties when, as with Irene, the parent herself makes the decision, the reverse is more frequently the norm. That is, the adult child initiates placement contrary to her parent's wishes. Joyce in chapter 10 did exactly that. She knew that for her marriage with Martin to survive, she would have to force the issue. What is interesting is that as of this writing, Joyce's mother has successfully completed the initial period of adjustment and is enjoying her independence and relationships with peers in her new home.

The ability of an adult child to communicate firmly and sensitively to a resistant parent that placement is necessary rests upon her maturity. If she can approach her parent with confidence, secure in her conviction that what she proposes is for her parent's and her well-being, her parent's response will be a positive reflection of her own solid belief and gentle authority. Under the best of circumstances, a parent finds it hard to accept the necessity of nursing home placement. The last thing a mother needs to hear from her daughter is a message, though meant to be reassuring, tinged with guilt and un-

certainty. A parent's anxiety and fear over placement are only intensified when an adult child is unable to demonstrate the support and
confidence required at this crucial time.

Visits to a parent in a nursing home are an effective way for an
adult child to combat feelings of helplessness and guilt. Nursing
home visits, however, are a delicate matter, in that if they are motivated by guilt, they will lack the affective quality that brings gratification to our parents and to ourselves. The norms governing rewarding nursing home visits are the same as those underlying the
other tasks we perform to bring comfort to our elderly parents.
These norms, or guidelines, provide the theme for this book. If anger or guilt is the motivating force for your visit, the purpose of the
visit itself—to bring happiness and a feeling of "you matter" to your
parents—is negated. You may be able to fool your parent into thinking you are emotionally with her, but the energy required to pull off
such deception is depleting. If this kind of charade continues, you
will eventually burn out, your parent will sense that something is
awry, and nursing home visits will degenerate into unpleasant
chores, lacking the warmth and genuineness essential to their
success.

Again, parents, even those in nursing homes (see chapter 2),
want to be part of your life; they crave to hear news (both good and
bad) of you and your children. If mentally intact, they have not
surrendered their passion for lively conversation to infirmity; indeed, because of added physical and social limitations imposed by
their new environment, they are more eager than ever to assume
roles of mentor and sage. Parents, whether in homes or institutions,
want to feel and to know they are still needed by their children. Even
parents suffering from dementia, who no longer know who and
where they are, respond with a sigh to a hug, caress, or squeeze of
the hand. Confusion does not blunt one's ability to feel. Children
who bear this special pain can still bring meaning to their nursing
home visits with nonverbal communication. The point is that we
cannot bestow these joys upon our parents if we are burned-out,
angry, or feeling guilty. Any of these emotions sap the spirit necessary for close, genuine encounters.

Emotional abandonment is far more detrimental than physical
abandonment to a parent's well-being. We do not emotionally abandon our parents by placing them in a nursing home if our visits to

them are rooted in love and compassion. We can remain their source of joy and connection to the world outside the institution.

The adult child must gauge for himself what he can and cannot do, so that he will have the energy to make visits meaningful. For example, the adult child whose parent remains angry will have a difficult, if not impossible, time infusing visits with affection and warmth. With hurtful barbs and negative comments to greet him as he comes through the door, he is well advised to visit infrequently, keep visits short, and listen rather than be defensive. Said one adult son, "My mother always tells me I murdered her by putting her in this home. That she's already dead and I don't care a whit for her. She constantly complains about the staff's injustices and neglects and the terrible food. I merely listen and tell her I can understand her anger. In the meantime, she has been at this home for two years and is gaining weight. Under these circumstances, I never visit more than twice each week—sometimes once is all I can take. She has been angry all her life. Sometimes I think it's her anger which keeps her alive."

In Irene's case, she initially visited her mother every day. Her visits were motivated by guilt and the sense that she had abandoned her mother. She continued these duty visits for two months and by the time she joined my support group, she was burned-out and angry and her husband was rightly concerned about her health. Again, with group support she was able to admit that most of her visits were not enjoyable, and she became aware that she was displacing some of her anger onto nursing home staff. She told us she always found fault with this aide or that nurse whenever she visited, and she was certain that the staff found her obnoxious and exasperating.

The "sorting out and exploration of feelings" process enabled her to change her behavior dramatically. For one thing, she stopped visiting as frequently. With visits sensibly spaced, she felt less pressured, and visits to Mother became mutually pleasurable and satisfying. As a result of the lessened visitation, her anger dissipated. The ultimate outcome was her improved relations with staff. They no longer ran from her when they saw her enter the building. With complaints couched in calmer tones and language they were responsive to her bidding.

Nursing home staff are perhaps the most underpaid and under-recognized persons in the health field. Their work is of infinite human value and they deserve whatever reward and recognition we can give them. The very least those of us who have parents in nursing homes can do is to give these devoted individuals the respect and courtesy they deserve. I personally do not think it inappropriate to bestow gifts to those aides and nurses who have shown extra kindnesses to your parent. Should this not feel right to you, then why not bring a basket of food or fruit to the nurses' station so that all can share? Even a note or card with words of appreciation can make an aide feel that what she is doing is worthwhile. Aides, especially, are the backbones of nursing homes and should be validated for their services at every opportunity. After all, what could be more important than the care of our mothers and fathers in their final years of dependency?

I do not want to dwell too long on nursing homes, for much of importance has already been written on this subject. Adult children must understand, however, that the first six months of nursing home placement are the most difficult and crucial. Until a parent settles in, and many sadly do not, the adult child will not only witness the painful adjustment of her parent to the inexorable loss of her home, but also struggle with her own feelings that are attendant to her parent's adjustment.

An important resource to utilize during the six-month period is the social service staff of the nursing home. Do not hesitate to talk to these professionals about what you feel is not right or bothering you. They will be happy to differentiate what is normal adjustment behavior from what is not. They will offer suggestions on how to help your parent through this transition. They will also have empathy for your pain. Many nursing home social workers run groups for adult children to aid them through this period of adjustment and to teach them the ins and outs of the nursing home system so they can be effective advocates for their parents. If these groups exist, join them. If not, suggest to the social worker that he form them. Tell him you would be happy to make phone calls and to assist him if need be. Become a nursing home volunteer. Such involvement will blunt your own feelings of helplessness.

The placement of a parent in a nursing home is always accompanied by pain and sadness. It cannot be otherwise. When the time arrives for the adult child along with her parent to make this hardest of all decisions, the thought that she could have and should have done more is unrelenting. Although she knows that she did the best she could, she is tormented by feelings of guilt and betrayal. Coming to terms with these crippling emotions requires effort. These feelings must not be denied but invited into consciousness so that they can be met head-on and mastered. A support group, composed of people who are experiencing the same emotions, is one of the most effective means to combat the loneliness, despair, and isolation the adult child feels at this time of loss. As a member of a support group, he knows he is not alone and that others exist who understand exactly how he feels. Help of this nature is infinitely healing. Additionally, support groups, as in Irene's case, can help the adult child expunge his guilt. By exploring and reviewing (over and over again) the realities leading to placement, the group gently and nonjudgmentally leads the adult child to the appreciation that his best was good enough.

For those adult children whose parents settle in and successfully make the transition from home to institution, the letting go of guilt is easier. For those whose parents do not adjust and die within the first six months or who live but remain angry and despairing, continuously pounding their visiting adult children with rage, the task of coming to terms is much harder. In these instances, group support may fall short of helping the child cope with her feelings of helplessness and frustration. Professional counseling may then be essential.

As pointed out in chapter 8, our parents are people with different personalities and patterns of adaptation. Some will successfully adjust to nursing home placement; others will not. The overall adaptation of our elderly parents to the built-in losses and caprices of life will pretty much determine their response to their new living arrangement. Although our emotional support, in terms of visits and involvement, does make a difference, it is one of several factors that influences whether a parent will settle in or not. The success or failure of placement hinges in large part on the inner capacity of that particular parent to adapt to change. Furthermore, parents who are emotionally healthy and resilient may consciously decide they do not wish to live this way and just die. Therefore, the adult child who persists in thinking she is totally responsible for any fatal outcome is assigning too much credit to herself and is also being needlessly self-punishing.

Remember, there does come a point when this hardest of all decisions has to be made; when you realize both you and your parent would be better served in a nursing home. Although I have worked with families who, at great personal and financial sacrifice, were able to provide good skilled care to a parent at home, they are the exception rather than the rule. Unless you have a whole corps of nurses, aides, and therapists within your own family, who are willing to be on twenty-four-hour call free of charge, you cannot take care of your parent without experiencing physical and emotional exhaustion and incurring extraordinary expense. Let no one tell you otherwise: nursing home care at one hundred dollars per day *is* cheaper than comparable home-health care. Home-health care around the clock can run twice as high. Nursing homes are not only equipped to give difficult and grueling personal and medical care but also provide social stimulation that cannot be replicated in a home environment. The value of a group experience, consisting of dining, recreation, and communication with others, cannot be overestimated. To get up each morning to the sounds and voices of people parading through their daily routines is emotionally healthier than to awaken alone in silence. Sitting in a lounge among others, whether one actually talks to them or not, is more reality orienting than spending a day in isolation watching images on a T.V. screen.

Nursing homes in this country have come under much rightful scrutiny and criticism. In my state, New Jersey, as a result of the Licensure Reform Law and the establishment of the Office of the Ombudsman for the Institutionalized Elderly, standards of care have risen and residents' rights are protected. For those who have parents in nursing homes, learn what the appropriate channels are and direct your complaints through them. If results are not forthcoming, follow through with letters and phone calls. Make noise. It is your right. Remember that whatever you can change or even bring to the attention of the appropriate persons may benefit you one day. You can make a difference!

Official reports on nursing homes are public information. In New Jersey these reports are available to citizens upon request from the state Department of Health.* Utilize these materials and other consumer information when selecting a nursing home for your parent. Your state Department of Health and Division of Medical As-

---

*The appropriate department may have a different name in other states.

sistance and Health Services (Medicaid) offers free, useful pamphlets to aid you in choosing the best facility. Do not be a passive observer. Find out all you can about specific nursing homes before placement, and whenever possible I urge you to take your parent with you when you visit. It is your parent's right to help choose his final home. The greater the role a parent can play in the selection process, the less powerless she will feel over her life. After placement, be assertive in verbalizing your grievances and complaints. The spin-offs of such efforts are enormous. You will experience less helplessness and guilt and consequently be a more loving, meaningful, and effective caregiver to your institutionalized parent.

For those who are considering nursing home placement for a parent, I recommend Nancy Fox's *You, Your Parent and the Nursing Home* (Buffalo, NY: Prometheus Books, 1988) as a helpful resource. It is concise and sensitively written yet filled with essential guidelines for long-term care.

13

The Second
Hardest Decision

As mentioned in chapter 1, most parents in old age prefer to be near their children. After spending active and satisfying years in Florida or Arizona, they return to their children's communities for the emotional support only families can give. Although such moves entail dramatic shifts in relationships, in that children who have lived apart from their parents for a long time are unaccustomed to few, if any, parental intrusions upon their time and space, more frequently than not both generations welcome the opportunity to be physically near each other again. Said one adult daughter, "Sure, it's different after all these years of being apart. But I am glad Mom and Dad are here. I was never really on top of things when they lived a thousand miles away and our last few visits together were not enjoyable, as I spent every minute trying to line up help for them. Of course, there are time sacrifices I have to make now, which I was not called upon to make before, but I am not resentful." Even when the adult child–elderly parent bond is not tight and the return of the parent poses emotional strain that did not exist at a distance, the adult child will usually say it is better to have Mom or Dad near.

But what about the parent who lives fifteen hundred miles away and does not wish to be near her children, not from anger or hostility toward them but because she does not wish to leave that which is familiar and because she does not wish in any way whatsoever to be a burden. As a frail, eighty-year-old widowed father recently said to me:

I don't think it is so good in these years for me to be too close to my daughter. She is wonderful and I love her deeply. But she has her own life and I do not want her to give up any of it for me. She has a successful career of which I am proud and I want her to continue to enjoy all that career brings her. Besides I have lots of friends in Florida, whom I am able to see every day. What would I have if I moved where she is? You know what would happen? She would drag me all over to meet people, so that I could have new friends. But you can't change horses in midstream and I would feel alone and eventually get depressed. She would feel responsible for me and sooner or later become angry that all that she is doing is not making me happy. I would get angry too, and that would be the end of our beautiful relationship. I tell her over and over again, I will not move to her town.

How does this daughter or any adult child deal with the pain and helplessness such a parental stance generates? What can she do to convince her parent that he would be better off near her? Should she even try? How can she, though, in good conscience allow her parent to live so far away, when all evidence indicates that he would have better care and more emotional security if he lived closer to her? Next to nursing home placement, the decision to accept that your parent will not move near you for the care you can and dearly wish to give, is the most painful.

Does acceptance of this reality, however, mean you cannot be a dependable caregiver to your parent? No, you can still be a dependable caregiver; you can still be filially responsible, but the boundaries of caregiving will be more limited. As pointed out in chapter 4, it takes two to make any relationship work. The parameters of the caregiving relationship are defined by what each can and will do. If the child is willing to assume caregiving responsibilities, but the parent is unwilling to accept them, it may or may not be possible to negotiate some kind of compromise, depending upon the reasons for the parent's position.

The type of parent we are exploring in this chapter chooses to remain at great geographic distance from his or her child, not for negative reasons, but because he or she knows his or her needs for independence, social connection, and the comforts of familiarity will be met by this choice. This parent is usually better equipped emotionally to let his child into the caregiving experience than the angry parent. By virtue of geographic distance, however, the care will differ in quality and quantity from that given by children who live near their elderly parents. Yet, the adult child can still be a dependable, loving caregiver within these new boundaries. The situation of an adult daughter, whom I will call Susan, comes to mind.

Susan is a forty-nine-year-old only child of parents who live in a retirement community fifteen hundred miles from Susan's home. Susan and her parents always enjoyed a close relationship, and until her seventy-three-year-old mother was diagnosed as having Alzheimer's, Susan and her family would make yearly visits to their home and her parents would travel north to be with Susan and their grandchildren in the summer. Because of Mother's dementia, Mother no longer remembers Susan's, her husband's, or their children's names, and visits have become nightmares, filling Susan with guilt and remorse. She has implored her father to move near them but he refuses to budge. He insists that he is managing nicely with five hours of home-health care daily, and that as long as he can get out to play pinochle with his friends a few times a week, he is really quite satisfied. He tells her too that he finds it deeply rewarding to care for his wife.

When Susan visits them, however, she reports a different scene. To the contrary, Susan feels her father is depressed and physically exhausted; that the home-health care they have is unreliable and inadequate, and she has serious doubts about how well her mother and father are eating. She also notices that on the few occasions when her teenage children visit, their presence has an immediate perking-up effect on both her parents, even on her mother, who is usually unresponsive. How much better it would be to have Mom and Dad in her town, where they could see their grandchildren frequently. Susan, a freelance commercial artist who is able to work from her home, has lots of time to give Mom and Dad the loving care they deserve and that she genuinely wishes to extend to them. Additionally, her husband is supportive of these plans. Yet, no matter how hard she tries to persuade Dad to move, no matter how often she outlines the right and sensible reasons for doing so, her father refuses to acknowledge her arguments. Susan, as a result, feels guilty, helpless, and sad over her inability to care for her parents. She feels she has not only let them down, but herself as well. It had always been her hope that she would be able to return to her parents in their old age some of the devotion and love they had given her through the years.

Susan is not totally helpless. She can still be a dependable caregiver, but not in the way she has pictured. Because she and her parents live at a great distance from each other, what she will be able to do for them will differ from those things adult children who live nearby can do. She will not be able to have Mom and Dad over for a meal or take them marketing or to doctors' appointments. She will not have the luxury of seeing them once a week or more, if she chooses. But she can call them more often, every day if she wishes, and in Susan's case, she realizes that she can even financially afford visits every six to eight weeks. Moreover, with her father's consent, she decided to hook up with a geriatric care manager (see chapter 1) who could assist her father in lining up necessary home-health services and from whom Susan felt she could receive an objective assessment of her parents' social, emotional, and physical well-being.

The distant caregiver can still do things of meaning for her parents. She can still demonstrate how much she cares with phone calls, letters, and more frequent visits. These gestures reassure parents that they are not about to be emotionally abandoned by their children. Indeed, the emotional capacity to love and care for a parent is no less diminished than if the adult child lived nearby. The imprint of warmth and genuineness remains on whatever the distant care giver can do. Though Susan's options, for example, may be limited by geographic distance, no one can question the quality of spirit motivating Susan's caregiving. Nor can anyone say that she is not a fully dependable, filially mature adult daughter.

What can the adult child, who does not have the money to make frequent visits and phone calls or to hire a geriatric care manager, do? How can she prove to a parent that she cares? How can she cope with feelings of helplessness and guilt when geographic distance prevents her from assisting in ways that have concrete value? Sadly, her options are more limited. Since they are, she must use fully whatever time she and her parents spend together. She must, in other words, make the hours count. Telephone conversations, precisely because they are infrequent and costly, become precious moments to share feelings, thoughts, and happenings. There is always so much to say and so little time to say it! Visits likewise assume the same poignancy. As I have repeated, emotional involvement matters more than concrete concerns. Although distance and money curtail practical things you can do, you can still let your parents know that you love them and how important they have been in your life. You can also reassure them that in any emergency or crisis, within your limitations, you will do your best to be there for them. Those parents who choose to remain in their distant homes understand your feelings. Your words of love and support are often enough to sustain them. After all, a central motivating force in their decision to retain their present residence is their desire not to be a burden.

With regard to concrete caregiving, there are nonprofit services available to adult children who cannot afford to hire a private geriatric care manager. Through a family service agency,* for a minimal fee or no fee at all, you can arrange to have a social worker periodically look in on your parent and then send you a report on exactly what is going on. In this way, if you have a hunch that Mother or Dad is not doing well, your instincts can be validated by a home visit from a professional. I must emphasize that such services cannot be provided unless your parent states it is okay. If your parent refuses, you cannot force visitation.

Much of my work at Jewish Family Service consists of home visits to parents whose children live far from them. I not only apprise children of their parents' welfare, but in time also become a source of concrete support to the parents themselves. After parents get to know and trust me, they will frequently call for advice with a problem, help in filling out a Medicare or Medicaid form, information on entitlement programs, assistance in obtaining a homemaker, or just because they need an empathic ear. The fee for these services is paid by the adult child or divided among cooperative siblings. At Jewish Family Service, like other accredited family service agencies, we determine fees on the basis of income and the number of people who live on this income. We perform many such services at no charge at all. County offices on aging also provide outreach services or can refer you to an agency or organization that does. Children of Aging Parents, CAPS,† is also an excellent referral source. As a clearinghouse for individuals and organizations serving families or relatives with aging parents, it has up-to-date information on caregiving re-

---

*See appendix D for a fuller description of FSAs.

†See appendix F for a description of CAP's services.

sources throughout the country. There are things you can do although resources and options are limited.

Adult children whose parents reside far away experience genuine anguish over their inability to render more care. Feelings of helplessness, usually countered by performing concrete tasks, remain intense and persistent. The practical care options available to the adult child who lives close are nonexistent for the daughter who lives in Massachusetts and whose mother resides in Florida. No matter how much the adult child can squeeze in during a week's visit, she is aware that the minute she leaves her parents' home, she relinquishes control over whatever happens thereafter. Emotional involvement, though the most meaningful in the repertoire of caregiving activities, is not adequate to give the distant caregiver the sense that she is doing something for her parent that really matters or that she is doing enough. Consequently, the acceptance by the adult child of limitations imposed by distance is nearly impossible.

An adult daughter, whom I will call Pat, whose mother lives in England, states that there is not a day that she does not wonder how her mother is doing. Whenever she is in the supermarket and sights a daughter assisting her elderly mother with marketing, she yearns to do the same for her mother; in fact, she tells me she cries. Recently her mother broke her hip, and Pat took vacation time to be with her. Although geriatric services in Great Britain are far more comprehensive and accessible than in the United States, and Pat knows her mother's care will be superb, when she steps on the plane for her return home she is nevertheless haunted by the feeling that she has abandoned her mother. She is an only daughter (with brothers who live even farther away than she), for whom the support of family in times of crisis is an important value. She has begged her mother time and again to come live in the United States, but Mother has consistently refused. When Pat married her husband thirty years earlier, her wise mother foresaw the possibility of these generational conflicts and outright gave her daughter her blessings to go on with her life. In fact, according to Pat, her mother told her in the most direct manner that her loyalty now rests with her husband. In spite of such maternal maturity, Pat still feels guilt and deep, deep sadness. On an intellectual level, she is able to accept "this is how it must be"; emotionally, it is not so easy. In answer to how she copes with her painful feelings, Pat tersely replies, "I do the best I can. That's all I can do."

Concrete care options are certainly at a minimum for the distant caregiver. Consequently, he must mobilize whatever resources he can and be creative in developing new ones. For example, whenever Pat hears of someone who is planning a visit to England, she will ask that person, depending upon how close she feels to him, to telephone Mother, to visit, or to drop a prewritten letter in the mailbox every day so that Mother can have the fun of being deluged with personal letters for an extended time.

The distant caregiver must take caution to prevent what I call "operation self-destruct." Because parental visits are infrequent, it is easy to fall into the trap of being so consumed with concrete chores that the more important aspect of caregiving, emotional involvement, is disregarded. My friend Jill, who visits her ninety-five-year-old mother in Arizona for two weeks each year, made me wise to this syndrome. In an effort to compensate for all she cannot do the other fifty weeks, Jill frantically plunges herself into a series of tasks, from baking, canning, and mending to recaulking the bathroom tub. Achieving perspective on this excessive activity, she realized that at the end of a week she and her mother hadn't even enjoyed a relaxed cup of tea together. Exhausted and resentful, Jill felt the real purpose of her visit—to spend quality time with her mother—had been undone by meaningless housekeeping chores. Time is extra precious when parents live far away. Although concrete caregiving tasks are of unquestionable value, they must take second place to human encounters that are rich in intimacy and love.

It helps to remember that even the caregiver who lives near her parent cannot be nor should be on top of things all the time. As I have repeatedly emphasized, allowing a parent to take necessary risks (see chapter 2) acknowledges her right as a human being to make choices. The opposite, infantilization, only diminishes the inner spirit essential to what we call dignity. To treat a parent who is mentally intact as an irresponsible child strips him of autonomy, which in old age, more than at any other time, is an important source of self-esteem.

In my work with the elderly, I have come across many distant caregivers. I have even considered starting a support group exclusively for them. They seem, however, to benefit sufficiently from attending support groups for adult children who are faced with the general problems of elder care. Consequently, I encourage distant caregivers to find out where such support groups are held in their communities and to attend them as long as necessary. County offices on aging, local hospitals, community mental health centers, family service agencies, and CAPS will know of their whereabouts. Remember, problems shared with others who are experiencing the same ones are always lighter and more manageable.

14

"Difficult" Parents

ADULT sons and daughters have frequently described their parents to me as "difficult": When asked what they mean by this word, their responses are generally in this vein.

"Well, you know whatever I do for my mother is not enough. Although I see her at least once each week, phone her every day and reassure her that I am available for emergencies, she is never satisfied with my efforts." Or, "Although I visit her every day in the nursing home and rub cream into every part of her body and bring her special gifts, she tells me I am not doing enough. There is always another demand to do this or that." Or, "She's a very lonely woman, for which I am sorry. But she expects me to provide recreation and entertainment. I have suggested that she attend senior activities—trips, card games, lectures—in her community. She goes perhaps once or twice; then tells me the people there aren't friendly, are snobs or the opposite, they're not good enough for her. She has a whole range of excuses for being miserable. She has a way also of making me feel guilty for enjoying my active life. She'll say things to me like, 'You're so lucky to have friends and be busy.' If I have free time, she wants a big chunk of it. She's just never satisfied. I do a lot for her. Do I get recognition or thanks for it? Absolutely not!" Or, "My father only wants to talk about himself, never me or my family. When he is not complaining about how terrible he feels—his stomach, his knees, his bowels—and how awful it is to be old, he dwells on how life has cheated him. He usually blames his prosperous brother or my late mother for how his life has worked out. He's difficult, all right. In fact he's impossible! He never lets up. The minute I come through the door he begins with his recitation of 'I's' and 'me's.'"

Only because women generally outlive men do mothers predominate in this composite. There are "difficult" fathers as well; their personalities consist of identical characteristics. Difficult parents, although sharing some traits with uncaring parents (see chapter 9), differ from them in one major respect. Their demands on their adult children are tenacious. They appear to have made an art out of continuous, self-serving harassment. Unlike healthy old parents who thrive on doing as much as they can for themselves for as long as they can, difficult parents want everything done for them, particularly by their adult children. These parents seem to go out of their way to be a burden rather than the reverse. They have enormous expectations of what their children should do for them. Insensitive to their children's needs and unable to acknowledge that their children have lives that do not include them, they are disappointed at every turn with their children's caregiving efforts. They can be intimidating in the force with which they inflict their demands; demeaning in their criticisms of sincere, filial support. Under such powerful persuasive assault, adult children often feel guilty, finding it hard to say no. They cannot seem to detach or separate from their parents' circumstances. Filial maturity, the desired goal, is unattainable. Children of difficult—self-centered, ungiving, dissatisfied—parents present special problems requiring additional guidelines and help. They are the caregivers who come to us the most burned-out, the most stressed.

Very often the difficult parent does not loom full blown until after the death of a spouse. Because a husband or wife was there to fill the difficult parent's needs, her negative personality traits were quiescent. When the spouse dies, the adult child caregiver is surprised over what has popped out of the box. A classic personality profile of such a parent, Mrs. L., was eloquently articulated for me by her daughter.

I really never knew what a difficult woman my mother was until my father died. In retrospect, I should not have been surprised. The handwriting was always on the wall. It was just that throughout my mother's life, there was always someone there to fill her insatiable needs—first her parents, then my father. I was off the hook until Dad died.

My mother was an only child. Although her parents, my grandparents, were not rich, they were able to give her whatever she wanted. She had nice clothes. They gave her piano lessons. She even went off to college for two years, unheard of in those days. She was especially close to her father: "I was the apple of his eye. As far as he was concerned, the sun rose and set on me." She would repeatedly speak of his praises with great pride. She had a childhood remarkably predominated by pleasant memories.

At twenty-five, she married my dad, who already headed a successful small business. Like her father, he gave her whatever she wanted. He catered to all her emotional needs—to be admired, to be reassured about *everything*, to be a listening post for all her complaints and fears. He would bring her breakfast in bed, whenever she had one of her headache attacks. I remember she was always terrified of being alone. She was also terrified of growing old and dying.

My parents had few friends because my mother had to be center stage and could only talk about herself. To this day, she absolutely cannot listen to anyone else. She is an attention addict; most people cannot stand to be in her company. Even my children find that she makes them angry with her always detouring the conversation toward herself.

Growing up as her only daughter, I was as solicitous of her as my father. My older brother was lucky. He rebelled and really cut off from the family. He, his wife, and children live three thousand miles away. I married someone whose profession is in the same town and here I am. Now my father is dead, and she is driving me crazy. Initially I told myself she was never like this—so self-absorbed, so immature, so demanding. But, of course, she has always been this way. She acts like a spoiled child, expecting me to be at her side whenever she's anxious, has a headache or is in the throes of some crisis, like when there were roaches in her apartment. And I have to be there instantly, immediately.

It's not that she's uncaring. She has provided me with many opportunities. She's generous with her grandchildren. But her life is so empty and she is completely unable to cope with anything. And she is unrelenting in what she demands of me.

Difficult parents are difficult persons. They were difficult before they became our parents and will usually continue this way until death. They are in essence parents with problems, or "problem parents," if you wish. We, their adult children, are neither the cause of their problems nor can we heal them. Although, as with Mrs. L., the "difficult parent syndrome" may emerge after widowhood, Mrs. L. and those like her were, in fact, always difficult—demanding, self-centered, attention-seeking—persons.

Old age, with its natural stresses and losses, intensifies those personality traits that have always been. Old age is not a special occurrence divorced from the rest of a person's life. One does not suddenly become old with a nasty, ungiving personality. Old age is bound up with all the periods that preceded it. The young or middle-aged adult who has no friends, who is querulous and demanding, who does not have gratifying relationships with children and family, becomes an old person in whom the same personality traits predominate. The young or middle-aged adult who enjoys intimate relationships, is generous of spirit, can take responsibility for what happens to her in life, and has an optimistic outlook, will have the same persona in old age.

Nowhere is the significance of early years in the context of aging more clearly delineated than in Erik Erikson's *Childhood and Society*. I recommend this classic to all caregivers, if only to learn of the eight stages of the life cycle as presented in chapter 2.[17]

The essence of this section rests upon the premise that since every person was once a child, infantile fears accompany him throughout life. The unavoidable vestiges of infantalism, says Erikson, which "endanger man's maturity and his works" are present at every stage of the life cycle and make their impress upon man's passage from one stage to the next. Since each stage represents a turning point or crisis for the person, the successful resolution of tasks in previous periods leads to success or failure in future periods or stages. By the time people reach their final life cycles (Erikson's seventh and eighth), if they have not developed sufficient "ego maturity" they will live out their remaining years in stagnation and despair, "becoming self indulgent, as if they were their own or one another's only child."

Difficult parents or persons like Mrs. L. were thwarted in their ascent to maturity early on. Because Mrs. L.'s needs were met by overindulgent parents, she was not able to develop the inner strength and coping behavior (ego maturity) necessary for the successful completion of later stages. With an indulgent husband to replace her parents, the destructive process continued. With little tolerance for frustration and without the capacity for intimacy, two prime prerequisites for healthy aging, Mrs. L. regressed to the role of dependent, attention-seeking child. Ill-equipped to cope with the inevitable losses of aging, her final years are spent in despair with "a pervading sense of personal impoverishment."

Unlike the elderly parent who becomes uncharacteristically manipulative or demanding, because she senses she is losing control of her environment or because she has heightened feelings of abandonment, the difficult parent has always been difficult. Her problem is constant. It is not caused by old age; it preceded old age. Adult children caring for difficult parents must understand this concept. As with elderly parents who suffer from a lifelong history of depression (see chapter 15), their adult children can do very little, if anything at all, to cure that depression. With difficult parents, adult children must likewise accept the limitations posed by a long-standing, deeply entrenched problem.

Although change is possible throughout the life cycle and I am the last person to rule it out, old people, unless highly motivated, are not apt to make significant personality transformations. Sometimes, however, a painful event, like the death of a child or spouse, can produce dramatic changes. Charles Dickens's memorable Scrooge is an example of a remarkable "about-face" in old age. Lest we forget though, it took *three* ghosts to change him! So it is we adult children who must make the accommodations and shifts. We must figure out what we can and cannot do in caring for difficult parents, so that we can feel good about ourselves as caregivers. However, how can we achieve filial maturity when the odds are so against us in these circumstances?

The adult child must recognize that her unending efforts to please her difficult parent, to accede to all her demands, are nonproductive. Producing helplessness, anger, and guilt, these efforts perpetuate a long-standing pattern that was and still is resistant to change. Running back and forth to Mother's house at her beck and call, taking her out for lovely meals and shopping excursions, doing and being all that she desires, will not bring you recognition or thanks.

Difficult parents are deaf to "mature" statements about the priority of your needs. Self-absorbed and operating on their own wavelengths, they tune out your pleas for fairness. Strategies that succeed with manipulative parents do not work with difficult ones. Difficult parents are not receptive to open dialogues. An adult daughter whose difficult mother attacks her with complaints when she comes for weekly visits has finally learned the only way to keep her cool is simply to let her mother talk. She also brings along her knitting, so that she and Mother need not have eye contact, and her hands can be busy. Sometimes she vacuums the floor. She says this kind of noncerebral activity is very steadying and advises others under similar circumstances to do the same.

You are not the cause of nor are you responsible for your parent's longtime personality profile. That personality was there before you were born and will continue throughout your lifetime and hers. You cannot change it. You can only accept it and accommodate accordingly. When your parent carps that nobody seems to care about her, all you can do is reflect her mood and say, "That must indeed be a terrible feeling." When your parent, in reviewing her life, blames her late husband or a prosperous sibling for the unrewarding path her life has taken, all you can say is, "Mom, you've certainly had some bad breaks." When your parent accuses you of not caring for her because you were unable to visit this week, all you can say is, "I know it must feel that way to you Mom, but I do care." When your parent demeans every aide who comes into her home and then tells you they're all no good and she wants new help, all you can say is, "I'll talk to them and see what I can do. You need help, Mom, and I'm sure we'll straighten things out."

You cannot be defensive. You cannot counterattack with, "You're wrong, you're imagining things, I visit all the time, it's *your* attitude, can't *you* try to be nicer." Such posture leads to open warfare, causing anger, guilt, and more anger. Your safest move is to listen and reflect back to her what she is feeling. You cannot redouble your efforts at being the good child. You cannot fill the pot, because it cannot be filled. I have witnessed adult children knocking themselves out to bring contentment and peace to their parents. It doesn't work, so save your energy. Set limits and stick with them (see chapter 3). To give more than you can results in the self-destructive emotions of anger and guilt. Remember, your best *is* good enough!

Perhaps resolution for the adult child rests in genuine compassion for his difficult parent. This compassion should be rooted in the understanding that this was the only way a parent could live out his life. A compassion molded by such knowledge is a basic component of filial maturity.

15

Depression and the Elderly

MANY elderly persons suffer from depression. According to authorities, it is among one of the most significant psychiatric disorders of later life.[18] Studies indicate that depression is prevalent in at least 16 percent of the population over age sixty-five. For those in nursing homes, this figure can be as high as 40 percent. Every year about ten thousand Americans over sixty years of age kill themselves.[19] Although the sixty-five and over age-group comprises a mere 10 percent of the population, it accounts for 25 percent of all suicides. Frightening statistics, indeed!

What is more alarming, according to Nancy Osgood, a national authority on the subject of suicide in the elderly, is that these numbers "represent a drastic under-reporting of the true incidence. The elderly can easily disguise suicide by taking overdoses of drugs, mixing drugs, failing to take life-sustaining drugs or starving themselves."[20]* Because depression (and suicide) in the elderly is a problem of major import, it is essential that adult children who are caregivers to their elderly parents have some basic knowledge about the causes, symptoms, and available treatments for this illness. Such understanding will enable adult children to more fully appreciate their parents' struggles for meaning and purpose in later life. In addition, information of this nature will help them see what they can realistically do to help their parents and what is out of their hands.

Old age is frequently referred to as the season of loss. Contrasted with youth and early adulthood, which promise new experiences, opportunities, and relationships, the years from sixty on are more

---

*See appendix E, for warning signs of possible suicide in the elderly.

often than not marked with increasing sequential and multiple losses. These losses restrict certain kinds of growth. Loss of physical health and stamina, for example, limit one's ability to travel, to pursue athletic or physical interests, to stay up late, or even to eat what was once enjoyed. Loss of friends and family to illness and death depletes one's network of social contacts, in turn heightening feelings of isolation and loneliness and robbing life of the pleasures of intimacy. Loss of job or career, essential to one's identity, creates feelings of low self-worth and purposelessness. Loss of income due to retirement curtails the enjoyment of leisure activities like movies, theater, sports events, and weekend outings. The old person perceives her world as inexorably shrinking and more and more out of her control. Painful awareness that time in this shrinking world is running out, coupled with the onslaught of these dramatic losses, is sufficient to make even the most mentally healthy old person feel depressed. In fact, persons who have never been depressed before can become so after the age of sixty. That the elderly are more vulnerable to depression than any other age-group is certainly not a topic for debate.

The young or middle-aged adult cannot possibly conceive of the loss of power and control over environment the elderly person experiences. With good health, ample vigor, and all senses intact, the young adult glides through the activities of daily living with nary a thought to the marvel that she can do these things at all. Brushing one's teeth, taking a shower or bath, opening a can of soup, getting out of a chair, being able to hear the doorbell ring or see images on a television screen, and pouring water into a teacup are all taken for granted. The young and middle-aged simply do these things, that's all.

The seventy-seven-year-old man with Parkinson's disease must ask his wife, if he is lucky enough to still have one, to assist him with most daily tasks. In essence, he is dependent upon another human being to help him get through the day. Such dependency can make one angry, depressed, and even despairing. One elderly man likened this loss of control over his environment to being a puppet, unable to move, to do, or even to live unless someone were present to pull the appropriate strings. Another, a stroke victim, told me he feels lost at sea, in a storm, absolutely out of control. All he can do is sit in his wheelchair in his apartment; he cannot steer another course. A woman of eighty, who always took pride in her tastefully decorated home, but since she fractured her hip is limited in what she can do, spoke these words to me: "What good is it, anymore? I sit here in my lovely living room like a lump. I cannot enjoy taking care of my treasured possessions as I once did. I have to tell the aide to do this or that and whatever she does displeases me. I feel so helpless and so angry. You know, I cannot even water my beloved plants anymore without making a mess. I know you'll think I'm overreacting, that I should be grateful for what I have, but I would just like to die."

How could you or I possibly empathize with the despair of these people? It's no wonder that in training persons who wish to work with the elderly, simulation exercises are utilized where trainees wear eyeglasses smeared with vaseline and have their ears plugged with cotton. Even arms, legs, and bodies are immobilized in an attempt to sensitize health personnel to what it is like to be old. However helpful these training programs are, in the final analysis they are games. When they are over, we return whole and intact to our homes and family.

The closest I personally came to understanding what the infirm elderly feel was when I had the flu last winter. Flat on my back for eight days, totally dependent upon my husband and friends to take care of me, I viewed this experience as a dress rehearsal for old age. For a suspended period of time, I was privy to feelings of anger, helplessness, and depression. I felt like a nonperson, a "blob," just as the above eighty-year-old woman had described herself to me.

As people grow old and their bodies no longer work for them, they become physically dependent. As they retire and make the transition from producer to consumer, they become economically dependent. As they lose cherished friends and family, sources of intimacy and affection, they become socially dependent. There are other dependencies as well. The point to be made, to paraphrase the noted gerontologist, Margaret Blenkner, is that old people become dependent. The dependency of old people is a "state of being and not a state of mind . . . not pathological, not wrong, in fact a right of old age."[21]

Therefore, interdependence—allowing oneself to be dependent upon others—becomes a sine qua non for old age.[22] Paradoxically, the more an elderly person can place trust in the kindness of strangers, the more control she will wrest over her environment. The elderly seventy-five-year-old who sits in her home day after day because she doesn't want to be seen being pushed in her wheelchair has neither the freedom nor independence of the person who can accept her need for help. An eighty-two-year-old woman I know who always received gratification from having friends to lunch and dinner is still engaging in this pleasurable activity because she is not embarrassed to ask her invitees to pitch in. Interdependence permits the elderly individual to widen the circle in which she moves and to do more within that circle. In a real sense, interdependence confers upon her the chance to be master of her fate. Elderly persons who cannot master this task are at higher risk for depression.

What is depression? Is there a fairly uncomplex definition or explanation of this illness? Depression is a disorder of mood.[23] When an individual is depressed he feels low, blue, sad, hopeless, generally "down in the dumps." Feeling tired, irritable, and without energy also characterizes the depressive syndrome. Loss of appetite, inability to sleep, and constipation are physical signs of depression. Persons suffering from depression generally do not feel good about themselves. They experience a drop in self-esteem manifested by negative, cognitive thoughts, about how "bad," "stupid," "ugly," or "inadequate" they are. Obsessive ruminations about past guilts and "should-haves" predominate in this kind of dysfunctional thinking. According to Dr. Aaron Beck,[24] director of the Center for Cognitive Therapy, the University of Pennsylvania, these cognitions are what cause depression. In other words, the negative thoughts we have about ourselves and the way we process them make us feel sad, blue, irritable, hopeless, and without energy. "The depressed person perceives his present, his future and the outside world in a negative way and consequently shows a biased interpretation of his experience."[25]

For example, a seventy-three-year-old widower who lives alone and has no children or siblings is frequently depressed. He tells me that he is a terrible, cruel person during these depressive episodes; that he deserves to have the lonely life he has; that he knows everyone in the senior residence where he lives hates him and is always saying terrible things about him behind his back. After presenting me with this negative view of himself and his current life situation, he always relates the story about the time he "put his dogs to sleep." He cannot forgive himself for "murdering" them and at heart thinks he is a base person whom no one can love. That these dogs were blind and riddled with cancer cannot be considered by him. Nor is he willing to examine the issue that as long as he kept them he would not be able to live in his present lovely senior residence. The more he obsessed on his dogs, the more depressed he would feel, and the more hopeless his future appeared in terms of having friends and a less lonely life.

Or take the seventy-five-year-old gentleman with moderate Parkinson's, who would not go to his club to dine with friends because he thought his condition would repulse them. As a result, he completely withdrew from the social life that once afforded him so much pleasure. In referring to himself, the deprecating words "ugly," "disgusting," and "diseased" peppered his vocabulary. Since Parkinson's by itself carries with it a strong depressive component, the addition of his own self-critical thoughts to the pot added up to a surefire recipe for depression. This particular person, with psychotherapy, eventually was able to learn that he was creating his own rejection; that in fact it was he who believed he was a turnoff to his friends; that his own negative, dysfunctional thoughts had molded the ungiving world in which he found himself.

A final illustration of how negative cognitions can cause depression and alter a person's life concerns a seventy-five-year-old widow, a genuine "people person" who stopped going out because of a slight incontinence of bladder problem. Turning down invitations from beloved friends and family to do things and go places, she chose to remain in her apartment for fear of an embarrassing episode. As a result of this withdrawal, she lost a rich source of gratification and became severely depressed. Although meticulous in her grooming and hygiene, she believed there was an odor about her and like the Parkinsonian gentleman thought she was "disgusting." On the few occasions when she risked going out, her anxiety level was so high that her incontinence was exacerbated, intensifying her negative cognitions and her depression. With professional help, again psychotherapy, she learned how distorted her thinking was. Moreover, she was able to utilize appropriate relaxation exercises for bladder control. Although her problem was certainly real, to use Beck's words, she had "catastrophized" and "awfulized" it beyond rational proportions. She was ultimately able to restructure her life positively; as a result, her depression disappeared.

Old people do indeed have lots of negative things to think

about—from the state of their health, to fear of dying, to whether they will be able to pay their monthly bills, to how long they will be able to live in their own homes. Although the gravity of these problems should not be diminished, they can color the way elderly people feel about themselves. They can generate self-critical thoughts leading to feelings of worthlessness, helplessness, and finally, crippling depression. For children who are caregivers, it is essential to know about these faulty cognitive processes that bring deep anguish to their parents.

Another explanation for depression, which has relevance in the context of aging, was postulated by Sigmund Freud years earlier. He defined depression as anger turned inward on the self. Considering all that could make the elderly angry—from their many losses, to dependency, to the presence of chronic pain, to the uncaring, demeaning attitude of our society—that they are not in a state of permanent rage and revolution is almost incomprehensible. That this anger has assumed the guise of depression in large enough numbers of the elderly to be labeled a national health problem, does make sense. It becomes crucial then that old people obtain the help necessary to turn their anger outward where it belongs.

A seventy-four-year-old single woman, without prior history of depression, whom I saw on monthly home visits, was, finally, after almost a year, able to confess how angry and jealous she was of her caregiving sister. The sight of her healthy sister coming and going daily to minister to her aroused feelings of anger and hatred she had never experienced. These negative emotions so eroded her spirit that she gave up using her walker and ceased going outdoors. Spending solitary hours in her wheelchair gazing out the windows, she succumbed to crippling depression. She told me her anger was so pervasive that it smote anyone, young or old, who was fortunate enough to have good health. Deeply ashamed and guilty over these feelings, she had kept them to herself for over three years. With reinforcement from me that her anger was normal and that verbalizing it was healthy, in time she felt better. With less energy wasted on anger and guilt, she again practiced walking and even resumed needlework, which she had always found gratifying. Although I do not believe it curative to encourage negative ruminations in depressed persons of any age, granting permission to the elderly person suffering chronic illness and pain to vent anger over her circumstances is an exception. Such verbal expressions shift the focus of anger from inside the person to outside.

A significant factor contributing to depression in the elderly is bereavement. Twenty percent of widows and widowers show depressive symptoms after the death of a spouse.[26] Some studies indicate that as many as a fifth of suicide victims are widowers.[27] Although bereavement is a normal response to the death of a loved one, in the elderly it assumes a more morbid dimension. Because the elderly widow or widower has spent a large portion of his or her life married and because the environment of the grieved spouse is bereft of the necessary social supports of family and friends, the bereavement period is longer, lonelier, and more intense. Normal bereavement is six months to one year. In an elderly person, it may last two years or more.[28] Adult children caring for a bereaved parent must be alert to the symptoms of depression. If possible, they must encourage their parent to maintain social connections; not to withdraw from their network of friends. Bereaved elderly need to talk about their lost spouse. They need to reminisce about the good times and the bad. The adult child, if possible, must provide some personal time for this special remembering. After all, who better is there with whom to share memories than a son or daughter who helped shape them?

Remember, however, and this is important, that there is only so much you can do to help your parent through this painful period. When mourning lasts longer than two years and it appears that your parent cannot or does not wish to let go of her grief, then it is time for you to convince your parent to obtain psychiatric help. If your parent refuses, you cannot force her to the doctor's office. You must respect her right to make choices (see chapter 2), risky as those choices may be.

How does the adult child recognize depression in her elderly parent? The detection of depressive illness in the elderly is not easy, as it may initially be masked by focusing on some physical ache or pain—for example, "my back hurts, my stomach doesn't feel right, there's a lump in my throat." When these complaints cannot be substantiated by medical examination, we immediately think their cause is psychological. Because of the frequency of illness in old age, we cannot be so quick to label the elderly individual "neurotic." Nevertheless, as Alex Comfort warns, substantiated complaints of ill health may be the first symptom of major depressive illness.[29]

It is important to emphasize that persons experiencing depression for the first time after the age of sixty and who do not have a positive family history for mood disorders are more likely than not to be helped by psychotherapy, in the form of individual or group counseling. Individuals who have been able throughout life to receive pleasure from a broad range of activities and people and who have found gratification in roles beyond their jobs are likely candidates for recovery. It stands to reason that those who have based their self-worth upon physical attractiveness and strength, ephemeral traits that fade with age, are more likely to become depressed. Without a sense of who they are (what Eric Erikson calls "integrity"),[30] firmly rooted in mental and social values rather than preoccupation with body state, they will live out their final years in despair, without meaning or purpose.

When the person experiencing depression for the first time also has chronic illness, the road to recovery will, of course, be strewn with more difficult obstacles. Chronic pain alone is enough to make one depressed—to cause feeling of helplessness and hopelessness. It is almost impossible to feel "up" and optimistic when one is beset with excruciating physical pain. Medical advances, such as biofeedback and relaxation exercises using visual imagery, may be helpful in these instances. Adult children caring for depressed parents who are experiencing intense chronic pain may want to investigate these new techniques.

The greatest medical discovery for the treatment of depression in the elderly are the SSRIs (serotonin selective reuptake inhibitors). Better known to us as Prozac, Zoloft and Paxil, they have fewer side effects than earlier antidepressants, while also lessening the symptoms of anxiety, from which many of the elderly suffer. Some of my clients, under the supervision of a psychiatrist, have been able to tolerate SSRIs for a year and longer. My own father, for example, has been on Paxil for over three years. He went into the throes of a corrosive depression when he first entered a nursing home. Unable to sleep and without his usual zest for food and people, he lost all reason to live. Within a month of treatment, he became his vibrant self again. Paxil was responsible for his dramatic improvement.

Adult children caring for a depressed parent who never exhibited signs of depression until old age can play an active part in helping their parent feel better. They can encourage him to resume interests and hobbies that formerly gave him pleasure. They can actively abet continued socialization by planning outings to which one or two of their parent's close friends is invited. They can encourage healthy reminiscence ("life review," see chapter 5) about the past. They can let their parent know at every opportunity how wonderful it is to have a parent like him and how much they still need his love, wisdom, and good company. When dependency is a critical element in a parent's depression, adult children must allow the parent as many choices as possible. In such an instance, infantilization of the parent is the worst option; the parent must be permitted to do as much as he can by himself and for himself.

Elderly parents with *histories* of depression and melancholia, on the other hand, are more difficult to treat. They may respond only for a short time to SSRIs or not at all. In such instances, a psychiatrist might recommend electroconvulsant therapy (shock treatments). The point is that adult children who care for those parents cannot expect to have much of a positive impact on the course of the illness. They can certainly be emotionally supportive, but active efforts similar to those offered by adult children caring for *first timers* will be of no avail. They must instead encourage their parent to obtain psychiatric help (see chapter 4, "Unrealistic Expectations"), with full realization that their persuasion may come to naught. If your parent is mentally intact, no matter how serious her depression, she has the right to make her own choices. Some old people, strange as it seems, who have been depressed off and on much of their lives, seems to build a tolerance for dysphoria. While their children worry, they manage to survive.

Nonetheless, it is agonizing for the adult child to witness her parent live out her remaining years in a depressed state, lacking the vitality to savor life. We helplessly stand by, wishing there were something we could do; feeling there is something we *should* do. Excessive enmeshment in a parent's despair, with unending and unrealistic attempts to make that parent better, can only result in the adult child herself becoming depressed. We have just so much energy. In giving care to our elderly parents, it is crucial to know where we can make a difference.

16

Honor Thy Father and Mother: Help and Hope

THE elder parent–adult child bond is strong and will remain so. From my work with hundreds of families, I am convinced that the next generation is as committed to caring for their parents as we to ours. Indeed, as we move into a world depersonalized by high tech and burgeoning bureaucracy, human relationships assume even more importance. The warmth and closeness that can be achieved only in families are to be treasured as a final holdout against being robotized ourselves. Is it any wonder that even in families marked with emotional coolness between the generations, when old age comes, elderly parents still turn to their children for whatever they can give them? Adult children, too, are compelled at this family turning point to complete their filial task with maturity and love. Mothers and daughters, who have been tearing at each other for years, will make one more effort at understanding and acceptance. Fathers and sons, who have communicated superficially, will anxiously move toward closeness. The desire to heal past wounds and to resolve old conflicts is inexorable, as each generation feels the presence of "time's winged chariot." That the aging of our parents is a crisis for the whole family is a given. That this crisis can be turned into an opportunity for growth for both generations is what we must hope and work for.

Although middle-aged children want to care for their parents in their final years, current forces or trends in our society deeply stress the elder parent–adult child bond. Dramatic changes in the role and function of the family have complicated the patterns of our major relationships. Women, for example, who are the principal caregivers to their parents, work and frequently manage households without husbands. Women who do not work are called upon in middle age to care for their grandchildren so their daughters can bring home additional income. Children in their twenties and thirties, for whatever reason, return home to live at about the same time their grandparents experience physical and mental decline. Both men and women, in an era characterized by increased opportunity for personal fulfillment, choose to return to school or pursue new careers and interests in mid-life. As a result, the response to a call from Dad to take him to the doctor tomorrow morning is no longer a simple one. With Daughter, perhaps having to attend a ten o'clock business meeting or perhaps having made plans to go on an all-day outing with her husband, what should she do? Where should she be? Who comes first? As one adult daughter said to me, "When I am taking care of my grandchildren, I feel guilty I am not taking care of my father. When I am with him, I feel I should be with them. There's simply no way to win. Either way I feel guilty and conflicted." Forty years ago that same daughter would have known exactly how to respond without batting an eyelash. These conflicts did not exist, because the multitude of options and responsibilities facing middle-aged children, especially daughters, did not exist.

The future of elder care in this country promises to be even more complex. Women are marrying later in life, many couples are involved in second marriages (forcing the issue of what stepchildren owe their elderly stepparents), many couples are opting to have no children, while some men and women are deciding not to marry at all. These developments will certainly impact upon the nature of elder care in the years to come. On a practical level, by the year 2020, books on filial behavior may be as commonplace as volumes on social etiquette, as future generations of caregivers sort out what is expected of them within a new framework of family forms and relationships.

It is complicated and confusing enough now, without speculating in detail about the future. Guidelines are needed to assist middle-aged children through the emotional turmoil created by this life cycle crisis. Middle-aged children need to know what they can and cannot realistically expect of themselves in their role as caregiver to their parents. If they try to do it all and be all to their parents, they will burn out as caregivers and squander whatever time is left in resentment and anger.

The aging of our parents presents us with one of life's most trying tests. It challenges us to grow up. It demands that we put aside old resentments and conflicts in an effort to become fully mature people. It bestows upon us precious time to conclude unfinished business. It gives us time to learn from our parents who they are and, from this knowledge, who we are. It gives us time to find out what "makes our parents tick" and perhaps to integrate their wisdom into our lives. It gives us time, finally, to see our parents as people, imperfect and human, rather than as figures to be feared or rebelled against. It is a time, as well, to recognize that some wounds between elderly parent and adult child cannot be healed and that acceptance and forgiveness as solutions are not second best. Above all, it is a time to demonstrate to *our* children by our actions that friendship, love, and respect can be achieved between generations.

I fully believe that our parents cherish and respect our right to happiness and fulfillment. After all, who is more able to appreciate the importance of living fully than an aging mother or father, for whom the finiteness of life is a most painful reality? Our parents do not want us to spend our last healthy years completely immersed in their care. Most parents I speak with, who are being cared for by their children, more often than not tell me their children are doing too much. They are anguished when they see their children overwhelmed with caregiving demands and tasks.

One mother, in the presence of her daughter, told me she would rather pay for a homemaker than have her daughter do household work. The daughter refused to hear, insisting that Mother didn't mean what she said and furthermore, *she* wouldn't be able to live with herself if she failed Mother at a time when Mother needs her services so much. Whom is she failing? Mother or herself? The expectation to care for Mother so completely was hers, not Mother's.

I suppose this daughter's unrealistic wish to do it all is related to Elaine Brody's findings, mentioned in chapter 3, that we must return to our parents the same total care they gave us as children. Of course, we know to administer such care is impossible, yet we are compelled to do it anyway. And as we engage in this irrational process, we heap large doses of anger and resentment upon ourselves. No matter how much we do, we feel we could and should do more—our labors are never sufficient. Consequently, sooner or later we begin to feel angry that we have no time for ourselves or for others whom we love and wish to be with. Sooner or later we begin to feel guilty about being angry. We label ourselves "selfish," deciding the only way to atone for harboring an emotion as shameful as anger is to push ourselves to even greater extremes of caregiving. How do we halt this destructive process of anger, guilt, and anger? The only way to restore some balance to our lives is to set limits upon ourselves and to recognize that care given out of anger and resentment is care diminished in quality and spirit.

So, what are some guidelines and rules to help adult children give quality care to their parents? First, the adult child must recognize that there is only so much he can do. The notion that he can do it all must be surrendered, must be let go, with full awareness that to run in all directions is to run no place; that to spread oneself thin is beneficial to no one, least of all to himself. Frenzied activity of this kind produces only superficial care; care without spirit or substance; care whose emotional foundation is anger, not love. Such caregiving, if allowed to go unchecked for long periods of time, will make the caregiver ill. The number of caregivers suffering from ulcers, backache, migraine headaches, and gastrointestinal disorders, not to mention depression and anxiety, has already been documented.

Adult daughters and sons who are caring for their elderly parents must, therefore, learn to listen to their inner voices, to psychic stirrings that signal anger, irritation, impatience, and resentment. If, for example, while waiting with your mother in the doctor's office for her appointment, you are gritting your teeth and feeling a familiar churning in the pit of your stomach because you are anxious about getting lesson plans prepared for the next day, or getting to the grocery store, then it is time to take stock of what's going on. It is time to listen to what your inner voices are saying to you. Are you doing more than you can handle? Are you beginning to feel stressed and burned-out from running in too many directions? Are you beginning to notice that you have less and less leisure time to enjoy? Are others who are important to you feeling deprived or neglected because of the large amounts of time you spend caring for your parents? When the answers to these questions are "yes," then it is time to steer a new course, which entails setting limits upon yourself, with the realization that you can still be a dependable adult child while doing less for your parent.

Second, we must remember that, by and large, our parents want to do for themselves as long as they can. As a result, it is vital that we ask them what *they* want from us and to respect their wishes. We cannot read our parents' minds. When we mind-read, as a rule, we end up projecting *our* expectations on to them, and usually create more work for ourselves. Do not assume that your parents require a specific service without asking them first. And *really listen* to their response to your question. Remember, too, that quality time with a parent is not defined by how often we see that parent but by how we feel about being with that parent at that particular time. We can not be with our parents emotionally if we are angry and resentful. Quality time can only be achieved if we have first taken care of ourselves by setting realistic limits on what we can and cannot do. We must let go of our irrational expectations that we can and should return to our parents the care they gave us as children. And if we really pay attention to what our parents are telling us, we will learn they do not expect such impossibilities from us.

Third, it is our right to ask for help from uninvolved brothers and sisters. If brothers and sisters live near enough to share responsibilities and have not, for whatever reason, ask them to do so. The worst that could happen is that a sibling will say no. To say nothing will not alter the situation. As pointed out earlier, a direct communication of what you are feeling in regard to their nonhelping stance may work wonders. If you are afraid to risk such a confrontation alone, then ask for a family conference of all siblings, led by a professional social worker or psychologist.

Fourth, although the potential to change exists at every stage of the life cycle, it is highly doubtful that our elderly parents can make major personality shifts. In some instances, acceptance of a parent's long-standing personality pattern is the only recourse. For example, with the realization that an authoritarian, controlling mother will not suddenly become "easy to get along with," we can learn to accommodate her traits, thereby reducing the tension in the relationship. Parents who will not allow their children to give them necessary help because they wish at all costs to remain parents is another painful reality with which the adult child must come to terms (see chapter

4). Understanding and acceptance of a parent's inflexibility as a way to achieve control over his shrinking world rather than as an act of personal rejection will alleviate guilt and anguish in the caregiver. Of course, such acceptance is risky! Your parent may not eat, take medication, or fall in refusing your assistance. Our parents, however, are not babies. They are adults, well aware of the involved dangers, whose choices we must respect.

Fifth, the importance, at this time of life, of learning to see our parents as people, not just as parents, cannot be overemphasized. The ability to perceive our parents as fallible, vulnerable human beings, no different from us, is essential to achieve full maturity and to aid us in objectively determining their care needs.

When we give up viewing our parents as people whom we must please at all costs, and begin to see them as "just people," we will more fully understand and accept their anxieties and fears. To look at our parents from this new perspective demands that we surrender our wish to remain a child and be cared for by them forever. Although the letting go of this fantasy ought to have happened earlier in our lives, our parents' old age presents us with yet another chance to complete this business. The irrational anger, talked about in chapter 11, that we experience when our parents can no longer do for us is a direct outgrowth of our wish to always be cared for by them. When we can finally accept that it will never be as it once was, that we cannot turn back the clock to that blissful time when our parents took care of all our needs, we have fully grown up.

Sixth, get help if you are feeling really stressed-out. See a professional social worker, psychologist, or other kind of mental health counselor. Remember, it is a sign of strength, not weakness, to ask for help when you feel you need it. Join a support group for adult caregivers, if this is your choice. Such groups are springing up all over the country. You can usually find out who is sponsoring them and where they are being held through your county office on aging or CAPS. Again, being a dependable caregiver to your elderly parents does not mean that you *have to do it all*, that you have to burn yourself out.

Although there is a serious shortage of home-health services in this country, one can usually find assistance if one tries. High schools, community and local colleges and universities, and vocational-technical schools are excellent sources to find people who care and need to earn extra cash. Calls to the personnel departments of these facilities are usually productive. Ads in newspapers, although requiring extra work in that respondents have to be screened, are also a fertile source of support services. Be creative in your search efforts. Remember, your own time is running out, so do not delay.

Through your local office on aging, CAPS or hospital, find out if your community has adult medical day-care centers where your parent could spend a few quality hours each day. These programs offer a nutritious lunch, medical supervision, activities, and socialization. They usually provide round-trip transportation. Above all, they provide you with a break!

Honoring our elderly mothers and fathers in Biblical times or even at the turn of this century was a dramatically different process than it is today. Daughters, for one thing, were not encumbered with multiple responsibilities, including jobs or careers. For another, their parents did not live long enough to require the prolonged care and rehabilitation efforts created by chronic illness. Ruth (a daughter-in-law, no less) was able to care for Naomi at no peril to her emotional and physical well-being. She was not a high risk for burn-out.

The definition of the verb *honor*, however, has not altered over the millennia. It still means to show respect for or to be a credit to. Of the many definitions in my dictionary, these at least make the most sense in the context of filial responsibility. What does it mean to show respect for or to be a credit to our elderly parents in today's complex, frenetic world? Does it mean that in the process of honoring them, we cease to honor ourselves? I doubt that then or now honoring our parents meant or even implied that we care for them to the point where we diminish ourselves as human beings. We cannot show respect for our parents if we do not respect our right to personal happiness. Likewise, I strongly question whether we can be a credit to our parents if we depreciate our need to take care of ourselves. We do not bring honor to our parents if, in caring for them, we allow ourselves to become ill. Nor do we bring honor to our parents if in caring for them we are angry and resentful. The guilt created by the unrealistic expectation to give total care to our parents strains, if not destroys, the elder parent–adult child bond. Knowing that our best is good enough will enable us to complete our filial business with maturity—with respect for our parents' needs and values and for our own. To honor thy father and mother ultimately means that we give up impossible, self-destructive expectations. Until we learn to honor ourselves, we cannot truly honor our elderly parents.

Appendix A
Offices on Aging

OFFICES on aging were established by the Older Americans Act of 1965. State offices on aging are located in state capitals in all fifty states. Local or area offices on aging operate in counties or designated regions. Telephone numbers for state and area offices can be found in the *Government Pages* of your telephone book. Typical services are as follows:

1. *Information and referral* on all community resources and activities for older adults. A written listing or brochure is available upon request.
2. *Outreach services* to isolated or housebound older adults.
3. *Nutrition services* at senior centers and Meals-on-Wheels.
4. *Assessment and case management services* to assess needs of elderly individuals, determine a plan to meet those needs, and coordinate services.
5. *Legal assistance* to older adults.
6. *Transportation*.

Some area offices on aging provide additional services such as protective services, homemaker services, counseling services, and chore services.

Appendix B
What Is a "Professional Geriatric Care Manager"?

THE professional geriatric care manager is an individual with a graduate degree in the field of human services (social work, psychology, gerontology) or a substantial equivalent (e.g., R.N.), certified or licensed at the independent practice level of his or her profession, who is duly trained and experienced in the assessment, coordination, monitoring, and direct delivery of services to the elderly and their families.

Services provided by professional geriatric care managers may include some or all of the following:

- Assessment
- Counseling
- Home care: assessment
                implementation
                long-term monitoring
- Crisis intervention
- Placement
- Care management
- Entitlements
- Advocacy
- Psychotherapy
- Education
- Consultation
- Information and referral

The professional geriatric care manager receives referrals from families (especially those living at a distance from their elders), from attorneys, hospitals, physicians, trust departments of banks, conservators, community agencies, employee assistance programs, and the general public.

Address:
1604 North Country Club Road
Tucson, AZ 85716
(520) 881-8008
Fax: (520) 325-7925

Appendix C
Levels of Care

1. *Short-Term Care*. Short-term care is provided in a rehab or nursing facility for up to ninety days. Short-term care is essentially recuperative in nature, following an accident (for example, a broken hip), illness (for example, stroke), or hospitalization (for example, post-surgery). Short-term care patients may be eligible for Medicare coverage when their care necessitates extensive, skilled rehabilitative procedures, such as daily physical therapy.

2. *Personal Care*. Personal care can be provided at home by a licensed homemaker or in a residential health care facility. Personal care consists of assistance with daily living activities—for example, bathing, dressing, personal hygiene, medication, and eating. Services rendered in personal care residential facilities are designed to promote and maintain the independence of residents.

3. *Intermediate Care*. Intermediate care can be provided within a nursing home for those with chronic, stabilized medical conditions, who have the potential to return home to their normal lives. Care at this level is restorative in nature. Intermediate nursing care is provided as well for those who do not have return-home potential and require more intensive, skilled supervision of their medical needs and daily living activities. At the intermediate level, residents do not require full-time skilled nursing care and are encouraged by staff to do as much as they can by themselves so that they can maintain a high degree of independence.

4. *Skilled Nursing Care*. This option offers maximum nursing care to residents who require twenty-four-hour licensed nursing supervision. Full-time skilled nursing home care is provided in nursing homes. Only these facilities offer comprehensive, long-term nursing care, maximum assistance with daily living tasks, and medical practices and procedures for life support. Skilled nursing care is a step below the level of care provided in an acute-care hospital.

Appendix D
Family Service America

FOUNDED in 1911, Family Service America (F.S.A.) has a network of 290 local member agencies throughout the United States and Canada. The membership includes accredited nonsectarian and sectarian organizations. F.S.A. is staffed by well-trained professionals and is the number-one source of professional counseling programs and other services directed toward the strengthening of families.

F.S.A. member agencies are nonprofit organizations governed by volunteer citizens from their communities. Agencies receive income from a variety of sources, including local United Ways and other fundraising groups.

One of F.S.A.'s many programs is service to assist individuals and families to solve problems associated with increased family pressures related to aging parents. These services include:

1. Support groups for caregivers to elderly parents and spouses.
2. Assessment and case management.
3. Individual and family counseling for persons involved in caregiving.
4. Information and referral.
5. Homemaker services.
6. Friendly visitor services.

For information on your nearest F.S.A., call or write to:

Family Service America
11700 West Lake Park Drive
Park Place
Milwaukee, Wisconsin 53224
(414) 359-2111

Appendix E
Patient Education Aid

"Warning Signs of Possible Suicide in the Elderly"
Nancy J. Osgood, Ph.D.
Postgraduate Medicine, Vol. 72/No. 2, August 1982

Family members and friends should become suspicious and call the doctor if any one of the following occurs in an elderly person.

- Change in sleep patterns, particularly insomnia.
- Change in eating patterns, especially loss of appetite.
- Weight loss.
- Extreme fatigue.
- Increased concern with bodily functions (for example, frequent complaints of constipation, loose bowels, aches and pains, dizziness, increased heart rate).
- Increase in amount of alcohol or number of alcoholic drinks taken.
- Change in mood, particularly if listless, apathetic, angry, hostile, nervous, irritable, depressed, sad, or withdrawn.
- Expression of fears and anxieties without any reason.
- Changes in behavior, especially episodes of screaming, hitting, or throwing things, or failure to get along with family, friends, or peers.
- Suspicious behavior (for example, going out at odd times of the day or night, waving good-bye or kissing good-bye if not characteristic).
- Sudden interest or disinterest in church and religion.

- Scheduling of appointment with a doctor for no apparent physical cause or very shortly after last visit to the doctor.
- Loss of physical skills, general confusion, or loss of understanding, judgment, or memory.

Appendix F
Children of Aging Parents
(CAPS)

Children of Aging Parents
1609 Woodbourne Road
Levittown, PA 19057

1-800-CAPS-294

CAPS goals and services:

> CAPS provides information and referral services throughout the country for caregivers.

> CAPS helps to increase community awareness of the problems of aging and caregiving through educational programs, workshops, and seminars.

> CAPS produces and distributes literature for caregivers.

> CAPS acts as a clearinghouse for individuals and organizations serving families with aging parents or relatives.

> CAPS provides individual peer counseling for caregivers through support groups and through telephone calls.

> CAPS publishes a national newsletter, *The Capsule*, with advice and current information for caregivers.

> CAPS provides employee assistance programs.

> CAPS helps develop support groups throughout the country.

> CAPS maintains a twenty-four-hour answering service.

To receive information through the mail, please send a self-addressed, stamped envelope to the CAPS office.

CAPS is a nonprofit 501-C3 organization. All donations and memberships are tax deductible.

CAPS membership is open to all individuals, professionals, and organizations who have an interest in caregiving of the elderly. CAREGIVERS CARE . . . AND SO DOES CAPS.

CAPS membership entitlements ($20 per year for individuals, $100 per year for corporations and organizations):

1. *The Capsule*: four-page newsletter
2. Networking-resources and information on a national level (when available)
3. Information on existing caregiver support groups—nationwide (when available)

Appendix G
Resources for Caregivers

Alzheimer's Association
919 North Michigan Avenue, Suite 1000
Chicago, Illinois 60611
(800) 272-3900

Arthritis Foundation
1330 West Peachtree Street
Atlanta, Georgia 30309
(800) 283-7800

Eldercare Locator Service
112 16th Street NW, Suite 100
Washington, DC 20036
(800) 677-1116

National Family Caregivers Association
9621 East Bexhill Drive
Kensington, Maryland 20895-3104
(800) 896-3650

Notes

1. E.M. Brody, "Women in the Middle and Family Help to Older People," *The Gerontologist*, 21, No. 5, 1981.
2. E.M. Brody, "Aged Parents and Aging Children," (Paper presented at National Conference on You and Your Aging Parents, Ethel Percy Andrews Gerontology Center, University of Southern California, 1978).
3. E.B. Visher and J. S. Visher, *Old Loyalties, New Ties: Therapeutic Strategies with Stepfamilies* (New York: Brunner/Mazel, 1988).
4. Daniel Yankelovich, *New Rules: Searching in Self Fulfillment in a World Turned Upside Down* (New York: Random House, 1981).
5. Christopher Lasch, *The Culture of Narcissism* (New York: Norton, 1979).
6. E.M. Brody, "Parent-Care as a Normative Stress," (Paper presented at Annual Conference, Marriage Council of Philadelphia, Division of Family Studies, University of Pennsylvania, November 1984).
7. Norman Cousins, *Anatomy of an Illness as Perceived by the Patient: Reflections on Healing and Regeneration* (New York: Norton, 1979).
8. David Riesman, *The Lonely Crowd* (New Haven: Yale University Press, 1973).
9. Alex Comfort, *Practice of Geriatric Psychiatry* (New York: Elsevier, 1980).
10. Madeleine L'Engle, *The Summer of the Great-Grandmother* (New York: Farrar, Straus & Giroux, 1974).
11. Robert Butler, "The Life Review: An Interpretation of Reminiscence in the Aged," *Middle Age and Aging*, Neugarten et al. (Chicago: The University of Chicago Press, 1975).
12. Ibid.
13. Elaine Brody, "All Generations Need the Gift of Caring," *National Association of Social Workers News* (March 1986).
14. Myrna Weissman, "Women and Depression," (Paper presented at Carrier Clinic, Bel Meade, New Jersey, June 1979).
15. Amy Horowitz, "Sons & Daughters as Caregivers to Older Parents: Differences in Role Performances & Consequences," *The Gerontologist*, 25, No. 6, 1985.
16. Irvin Yalom, *The Theory and Practice of Group Psychotherapy* (New York: Basic Books, 1985).
17. Erik Erikson, *Childhood and Society* (New York: Norton, 1963).
18. Fred Charatan, "Depression and the Elderly: Diagnosis and Treatment," *Psychiatric Annals*, 15/5 (May 1985).
19. M. Miller, *Suicide After Sixty: The Final Alternative* (New York: Springer, 1979).
20. Nancy Osgood, "Suicide in the Elderly: Are We Heeding the Warnings," *Postgraduate Medicine*, Vol. 72/No. 2 (August 1982).

21. Margaret Blenkner, "The Normal Dependencies of Aging," *The Dependencies of Aging* (Occasional Papers in Gerontology No. 6, Institute of Gerontology, the University of Michigan–Wayne State University, August 1969).

22. Erik Erikson, *Vital Involvement in Old Age* (New York: Norton, 1986).

23. *Diagnostic and Statistical Manual of Mental Disorders*, 3d ed. (American Psychiatric Association, 1981).

24. Aaron Beck et al., *Cognitive Therapy of Depression* (New York: Guilford, 1979).

25. Ibid.

26. Shirley Bromberg and Christine Cassel, "Suicide in the Elderly: The Limits of Paternalism," *Journal of the American Geriatrics Society*, Vol. 31, No. 11 (November 1983).

27. Ibid.

28. Alex Comfort.

29. Ibid.

30. Erik Erikson, 18.

Index

Abandonment and anxiety, parents' feelings of. *See* Anxiety and abandonment, parents' feelings of
Alcoholics Anonymous, 104
Alzheimer's disease, examples of, 17, 44, 77, 80, 105, 121
Anatomy of an Illness (Cousins), 27
Anger and resentment, children's feelings of, 37–39, 147–149; in children who have not achieved separation leading to adulthood, 72, 150; difficult parents and, 131, 132; manipulative parents and, 65–67; nursing home placement and, 109–111; pressure to pretend what you do not feel, 84; spousal priority and, 88, 89, 92–93, 95; support groups and unexplained, 100–104; suppressed, 101; understanding of, 78, 104; unexplained, 99–104, 150
Anger and resentment, parents' feelings of, 82, 83; depression caused by, 140–141
Antidepressant medications, 37, 143
Anxiety and abandonment, parents' feelings of, 11–14, 63, 65, 66, 82, 83; hospitals and, 76; nursing homes and, 112–113
Arthritis, 34, 83

Beck, Aaron, 138, 139
Bereavement upon death of spouse, 141
Blenkner, Margaret, 137
Brody, Elaine, 2, 22, 79, 91, 147
Brookdale Center on Aging, 96
Brothers and sisters. *See* Siblings
Butler, Robert, 49

CAPS. *See* Children of Aging Parents
Care, levels of, 157
Care managers, private geriatric. *See* Private geriatric care managers
Carlin, Vivian, 16
Center for Cognitive Therapy, The University of Pennsylvania, 138

Child care and elder care, difference between, 31, 45–49
Childhood and Society (Erikson), 130
Children of Aging Parents (CAPS), 126; basic description of, 123–124; detailed description of, 163–164; source of information on, 163
Clergy, counseling from, 98; support groups and, 104
Comfort, Alex, 44, 142
Conferences, family, 51, 54–55, 61, 149
Confusion and disorientation, examples of, 48–49, 77, 109, 112, 121; Alzheimer's disease, examples of, 17, 44, 77, 80, 105, 121
CONTACT (telephone reassurance answering service), 26
Cooking, parents and, 15, 34
Counseling: clergy, 98, 104; depression and, 37, 139, 141–143; family conferences, 51, 54–55, 61, 149; guilt and, 80, 115; manipulative parents and, 65; nursing home placement and, 115; psychologists, 22, 51, 54–55, 62, 91–92, 98, 104, 150; psychotherapy, 74–75, 139, 141–143; social workers, 22, 51, 54–55, 62, 91–92, 98, 104, 114, 150; spousal priority and, 91–95, 98. *See also* Support groups
Couple relationship, the. *See* Spousal priority
Cousins, Norman, 27

Death of a parent: children's grief upon, 105–106; remaining spouse's grief upon, 141; when the remaining spouse becomes a difficult parent, 128–129, 130
Depression: 48, 83, 121; antidepressant medications and, 37, 143; causes of, 135–143; children's attempts to cure, 36–37, 141, 142–143; counseling and, 37, 139, 141–143; definitions of depression, 138, 140;

Depression—(*continued*)
electroconvulsant therapy and, 143;
limitations on what can be done for,
131, 141; parents with a history of,
143; psychotherapy and, 139, 141–
143; reminiscence and, 40–41;
statistics on, 135; studies of women,
87; suicide and, 135, 141; symptoms
of, 138, 141–142
Diabetes, 83
Dickens, Charles, 131
Difficult parents, 84; aging's effect on
personality of, 130–132; caused by the
death of a spouse, 128–129, 130;
compassion for, 133; descriptions of,
127–132; limitations on what can be
done for, 131–133; visits to, 132
Disorientation and confusion, examples
of. *See* Confusion and disorientation,
examples of
Distance, parents and geographic. *See*
Long-distance care giving
Driving, parents and, 14–15

Electroconvulsant therapy, 143
Erikson, Erik, 130, 142

Family: definition of, 4–5; involvement of
parents in family matters, 17–18, 112;
nuclear, 4; remarried, 4–5
Family conferences, 51, 54–55, 61, 149
Family Service Agencies (FSAs), 126;
basic description of, 123; social
workers at, 123
Family Service America (F.S.A.), detailed
description of, 159
Financial matters, parents and, 15
Fox, Nancy, 117
Freud, Sigmund, 140
Future of elder care, 146

Gender: guilt and, 28–29; men as inner
directed, 28–29; siblings and, 58;
support groups and, 28–29, 58, 60;
women as other directed, 28–29, 97–
98
Geriatric assessment/evaluation units, 80–
81
Geriatric care managers, private. *See*
Private geriatric care managers
Grief, children's: upon a parent's death,
105–106; upon placing a parent in a
nursing home, 2, 77, 105–110
Grief, parent's, upon death of spouse, 141

Guilt, children's feelings of, 22, 23–24,
37–39, 64, 95, 148, 150; in children
who have not achieved separation
leading to adulthood, 72; in children
whose parents are geographically
distant, 121, 122, 124–125; counseling
and, 80, 115; difficult parents and,
128, 131, 132; gender and, 28–29;
manipulative parents and, 64, 67, 68–
69; nursing home placement and, 109–
113, 115, 117; pressure to pretend
what you do not feel, 84

Holiday seasons, 12
Home-health care: nursing homes versus,
116; sources of information on, 150–
151
Horowitz, Amy, 96–97
Hospital(s), 19; discharge from, 12–13;
medic alert systems and, 26; parents'
anxiety about, 76
Household chores, parents and, 9, 34
Husband-wife relationship. *See* Spousal
priority

Incontinence, 46–47, 77, 107
Independence of parents, 46, 92–93, 128,
149; cooking, 15, 34; depression
caused by loss of, 136–138, 142–143;
driving, 14–15, 35; financial matters,
15; household chores, 9, 34; when
they are geographically distant, 120,
125
Information, sources of. *See* Sources of
information
Inner directed, men as, 28–29
Intermediate care, detailed description of,
157

Jewish Family Service of the Delaware
Valley, 6, 123
Juggling of responsibilities, 22–23

Lasch, Christopher, 6–7
L'Engle, Madeleine, 46–47
Letters to parents who are geographically
distant, 122, 125
Levels of care, 157
Life care facilities, basic description of,
15–17
Life review, 49
Limits, setting: difference between elder
care and child care, 31, 45–49;
guidelines in, 33–41; importance of,
19–21, 148–149; manipulative parents
and, 63–69, 77–78; process of, 21–31

Listening and talking, 9–10
Loneliness, 11, 82, 136; manipulative parents and, 63, 66
Long-distance care giving, 5–6; independence of parents and, 120, 125; letters, 122, 125; parameters of the relationship, 120–125; reasons why parents choose to remain geographically separated from their children, 119–121; services available for, 123–124; support groups and, 125–126; telephone calls, 122–123, 125; visits, 122, 124, 125
Longevity, effects of increased, 3

Manipulative parents: aging's effect on personality of, 63, 64; basic description of, 63; counseling and, 65; setting limits with, 63–69, 77–78; support groups and, 68
Married life. See Spousal priority
Medic alert systems, 26
Medicaid, 123
Medicare, 123
Memory impairment, 14–15; Alzheimer's disease, examples of, 17, 44, 77, 80, 105, 121
Migration of parents, reverse, 6
Mount Sinai Hospital and Medical School, Department of Gerontology of, 49

National Association of Private Geriatric Care Managers, 6, 156
New Jersey, regulation of nursing homes in, 116
Nuclear family, 4
Nursing home(s): agreement among children over placing a parent in a, 60–61; anger and resentment of children upon placing a parent in a, 109–111; counseling and children's feelings about, 115; disagreement among children over placing a parent in a, 54, 77; disagreement between spouses over placing a parent in a, 93–95; grief of children upon placing a parent in a, 2, 77, 105–110; guilt feelings of children upon placing a parent in a, 109–113, 115, 117; home-health care versus, 116; New Jersey regulation of, 116; parents' feelings of anxiety and abandonment about, 112–113; period of adjustment in, 114, 115; placement decision as a difficult and painful one, 105–117; range of children's concern about, 4; skilled nursing care, detailed description of, 157; social workers in, 114; sources of information on, 116–117; spousal support and, 111; support groups and, 111, 113, 115; staff of, 113–114; visits of children to, 24, 44, 79–80, 109, 112–113; when the parent makes his or her own decision regarding placement, 107–108, 111, 117

Offices on Aging, state/county/local, 123, 126, 150, 151; what they offer and how to find them, 153
Osgood, Nancy J., 135, 161–162
Other directed, women as, 28–29, 97–98

Parkinson's Disease: depression and, 139; examples of, 19, 46, 75, 88, 136, 139
Pastoral counselors. See Clergy, counseling from
Personal care, detailed description of, 157
Personality, effect of aging on, 20, 40–41, 149–150; difficult parents and, 130–132; manipulative parents and, 63, 64; Scrooge as an example of personality change, 131
Phone calls. See Telephone calls
Postgraduate Medicine, 161
Private geriatric care managers, 122; basic description of, 6; list of services provided by, 155; qualifications of, 155; source of information on, 156
Psychologists, 22, 62, 150; family conferences and, 51, 54–55, 149; spousal priority and, 91–92; support groups and, 104
Psychotherapy, 74–75; depression and, 139, 141–143

Quality time, 10–11

Remarried family, 4–5
Reminiscence, parents and: healthy, 40, 49–50; as life review, 49; negative and destructive, 40–41
Reminiscence, siblings and, 61–62
Resentment, children's feelings of. See Anger and resentment, children's feelings of
Resentment, parents' feelings of. See Anger and resentment, parents' feelings of
Resistance. See Stubbornness
Respite care services, 27

Reverse migration of parents, 6
Riesman, David, 28
Role reversal: as a consequence of
    separation leading to adulthood, 72;
    false definition of, 43–44; what it
    actually means, 44–50, 78

Sandwich generation, 2
Scrooge, as an example of personality
    change, 131
Separation leading to adulthood, process
    of, 72, 89, 94, 150
Short-term care, detailed description of,
    157
Siblings: family conferences and, 51, 54–
    55, 61, 149; gender and, 58; involved
    versus uninvolved, 51–54, 149;
    parent's choice of, 58–59, 61;
    relationships among, 51–62;
    reminiscence and, 61–62
Sisters and brothers. *See* Siblings
Skilled nursing care, detailed description
    of, 157
Social workers, 22, 62, 150; family
    conferences and, 51, 54–55, 149; at
    Family Service Agencies, 123; in
    nursing homes, 114; spousal priority
    and, 91–92; support groups and, 104
Sources of information: on Children of
    Aging Parents (CAPS), 163; on
    Family Service America (F.S.A.), 159;
    on home-health care, 150–151; on
    nursing homes, 116–117; on Offices
    on Aging, 153
Spousal priority, 87–98; anger and
    resentment and, 88, 89, 92–93, 95;
    counseling and, 91–95, 98; emotional
    support offered by spouse, 95–97,
    111; nursing homes and, 93–95,
    111; separation leading to adulthood
    and, 89, 94; support groups and,
    94, 95
Stanford University, 102
State Department of Human Services, 17
State Office on Aging, 17

Stubbornness, 19–20; how to deal with,
    34–35
Suicide: attempts to disguise, 135; death
    of a spouse as a cause of, 141;
    depression and, 135, 141; statistics on,
    135; warning signs of, 161–162
Summer of the Great-Grandmother, The
    (L'Engle), 46
Support groups, 21–22; clergy and, 104;
    confidentiality of, 104; gender and,
    28–29, 58, 60; kinds of, 103–104;
    long-distance caregiving and, 125–126;
    manipulative parents and, 68; nursing
    homes and, 111, 113, 115;
    psychologists and, 104; social workers
    and, 104; spousal priority and, 94, 95;
    unexplained anger and resentment
    and, 100–104; universality of, 102–103

Talking and listening, 9–10
Telephone calls, 10–11, 12; long-distance
    caregiving and, 122–123, 125

University of Pennsylvania, The Center
    for Cognitive Therapy of, 138

Vacation, children's, 12
Visits of children to nursing homes, 24,
    44, 79–80, 109; guidelines for, 112–
    113
Visits of children to parents: to difficult
    parents, 132; to parents who are
    geographically distant, 122, 124, 125

"Warning Signs of Possible Suicide in the
    Elderly" (Osgood), 161–162
Weissman, Myrna, 87
Wife-husband relationship. *See* Spousal
    priority

Yale University, 87
Yalom, Irvin, 102
Yankelovich, Daniel, 6–7
You, Your Parent and the Nursing Home
    (Fox), 117

About the Author

VIVIAN E. Greenberg, A.C.S.W, L.C.S.W., is a graduate of Bryn Mawr College, the Graduate School of Social Work and Social Research. She is the author of *Should Mom Live With Us?*, written with Dr. Vivian Carlin, and *Children of a Certain Age*. She is currently in private practice in Pennington, New Jersey, and is a featured columnist in *Answers*, a magazine for adults with aging parents. She has appeared on *Oprah*, CNN's *Sonya Live*, and NPR. She conducts workshops and lectures throughout the country on the stresses of caregiving and the relationship problems between middle-aged adults and their elderly parents. She is also the daughter of a ninety-four-year-old father, Arthur, for whom she is the primary caregiver and who happily resides in a nursing home.